DATE DUE

The Substance of Hope

THE
SUBSTANCE OF
HOPE

Barack Obama and the Paradox
of Progress

WILLIAM JELANI COBB

Walker & Company
NEW YORK

Published by Walker Publishing Company, Inc., New York

All papers used by Walker & Company are natural, recyclable products made
from wood grown in well-managed forests. The manufacturing processes
conform to the environmental regulations of the country of origin.

LIBRARY OF CONGRESS CATALOGING-IN-PUBLICATION DATA
HAS BEEN APPLIED FOR.

ISBN: 978-0-8027-1739-9

Visit Walker & Company's Web site at www.walkerbooks.com

First U.S. edition 2010

1 3 5 7 9 10 8 6 4 2

Typeset by Westchester Book Group
Printed in the United States of America by Worldcolor Fairfield

For my nephews William, Terence, and Tymel:
Hope audaciously, work relentlessly.

Now faith is the substance of things hoped for, the evidence of things not seen.

Hebrews 11:1

Contents

CHAPTER 1

Forty-four

THE MEANING OF BARACK OBAMA

ON JANUARY 20, 2009, a black man stood on the steps of the U.S. Capitol, placed his hand on a Bible held by his wife, and was sworn in as president of the United States. I was there that day, frozen nearly solid but still awed by the magnitude of what I had witnessed—nothing less than the passing of an old era and the initiation of another. I was born in August 1969, sixteen months after Martin Luther King Jr. took his fateful step onto that balcony in Memphis. I am part of that generation reared in the seemingly permanent shadow of King's life and the violent way it ended. I have often taken solace in that speech he gave on April 3, 1968, the one where he seemed to dip his toe into the waters of his own mortality as if he somehow knew that he would soon be fully immersed. In that speech he uttered his contralto prediction that "we as a people will get to the Promised Land." Since then, at points when our community prospects seemed most bleak, many of us have fallen back on those words, believing that a man who saw his own fate so clearly was capable of seeing ours also. For many, that inauguration day in 2009 was validation of King's promise.

For the entirety of this nation's history the phrase *black president* had been a contradiction in terms, but in the course of a forty-two-word oath, its terms were reconciled. The moment was not simply about words—that was only one of many reconciliations both grand and minute. Consider this: In 1908 Jack Johnson defeated a white man for the heavyweight championship, and race riots erupted in the streets across the country. One hundred years later Barack Obama defeated a white man for the presidency, and the streets were filled with riotous laughter as millions of people simultaneously broke into the Electric Slide.

In addition to bearing the burdens that come with the presidency, Barack Obama is freighted with the vast weight of his own symbolism. His position is so unique and so far outside our expectations as to make him a metaphor for a metaphor. It is possible, almost unavoidable, to see Obama's entire life—from birth to inauguration—as a referendum on civil rights causes. This biracial black lawyer who relied on millions of black voters to help him win the presidency serves as an unmistakable reminder of the NAACP's legal battles to end the "white primary" in the 1930s, its campaign to end segregation in law schools in the 1940s, the *Brown v. Board of Education* decision in 1954, and the Voting Rights Act of 1965. Without the civil rights movement, the marriage of Barack Obama's African father and his white American mother would have been illegal in most states of the South.

The headline for the *New York Times* on November 5, 2008, blared from the page: RACIAL BARRIER FALLS IN DECISIVE VICTORY. Obama's name appeared in ninety-six-point type. Only three events in the paper's history—the Apollo landing, Richard Nixon's resignation, and September 11 attacks—were heralded with equal dimensions. At Ebenezer Baptist, the church once pastored by Martin Luther King Jr., the congregation gathered for a Watch Night service. It was a deliberate recasting of history, an echo of those slaves who gathered on the last day of 1862 awaiting New Year's—the day the Emancipation Proclamation would take effect. In Nairobi entire communities stayed up throughout the night, anticipating the moment when one of their own descendants would be declared the new president. And in Grant Park in Chicago seven hundred thousand people jammed into the space along Lake Michigan to hear Barack Obama say, "Change has come to America."

And it has. But the dimensions and contours of that change are not yet apparent. We will not know its full yield, the ways in which it will alter race and citizenship and possibility, for many years to come.

In the meantime we have filled that space with the metaphors. The American creed of "Out of many, one" has been turned on its head, a character defined by the ideal of "Out of one, many." Barack Obama is the black president and thus the American Mandela, the yield of a once-enslaved people's aspirations toward freedom. He is a biracial man with family members on four continents—and therefore is the face of the next generation, one that is multiracial and cosmopolitan. His family is a testament to globalism. He is the Democrat who won 53 percent of the popular vote and thus is the punctuation at the end of the Reagan Era. His policies defy the traditional categories of liberal or conservative, thus heralding the end of the tread-worn arguments over the 1960s culture wars. He is shorthand for celebrity, for digital politics, for change and for hope. And somewhere, beneath all that, is a human being who happens to be the forty-fourth president of the United States.

There are other metaphors. A century ago W. E. B. Du Bois published an essay titled "Of the Meaning of Progress" in his collection *The Souls of Black Folk*, in which he recounted his days as a teacher in small-town Tennessee. More than a summer job, his task, as he saw it, was part of a monumental undertaking to uplift the race. Ten years after leaving the town, he returned, now a respected professor and the first black man with a Ph.D. from Harvard, but he found that the progress had not been uniform. Some of his former students had died unexpectedly, while others remained mired in conditions scarcely better than slavery. Du Bois's own accomplishments marked a step forward for the black community, but what that meant in the context of the times was hard to interpret precisely. There. Another metaphor, another attempt at bringing light to a circumstance so novel as to be a source of both inspiration and confusion. Obama's election represents progress, its meaning as complex and cryptic as life in Du Bois's Tennessee town.

It is difficult, in fact, to read *Dreams from My Father* without hearing other echoes from *Souls of Black Folk*. The Harvard-educated black president had an unwitting kinship with the Harvard-educated black scholar. Both men grew up fatherless in environments where blacks were a small minority. Both men's searches for identity were intricately bound to their ability to decipher the meaning of race. In the early pages of his memoir Obama tells of a haunting a magazine image of a black man who has bleached his skin, in a failed attempt to come closer to whiteness. It becomes a moment of reckoning for him. Du Bois spoke of the point in his childhood when a playmate rejected his friendship and the difference of his skin first dawned on him. These tales are compelling precisely because they are typical. In a society where race is as ambient as air, such moments are usually the hard but regular features of life, not the beginnings of existential journeys.

As a young man, Du Bois left his childhood home in Great Barrington, Massachusetts, for Tennessee and Fisk University. There he first encountered black communities, came to understand black culture, and began to grapple with its implications for his own life. Obama began college in California but then transferred to Columbia University, in part because of its proximity to Harlem. Later Chicago's South Side came to serve for Obama the functions that Nashville had for Du Bois—a literal starting place within black America. Their unique experiences made both men variables in the racial equation. Du Bois lived ninety-five years, authored volumes of history, and became the godfather of the civil rights movement. Obama's meaning to race and democracy in this country has yet to be charted, which perhaps more than anything else is the reason we find the story of 2008 compelling. Beneath all the celebration, the commentary, and the joyous merchandising of an American moment, lies this unanswered question: What is the meaning of this progress?

The man who became president waged a twenty-two-month campaign against cynicism. It was a clever bit of wordplay. Had he railed against racism, he would have found himself exiled to the fringes—Al Sharpton territory. Even the most righteous mention of discrimination would likely have alienated white voters. But cynicism was fair game. Your doubts about a black man becoming president weren't *racist*—they were cynical. None of the old deflections, none of the head fakes or portable indignations, came into play. No talk-radio hosts advocate cynicism. No black leaders picket against it. If the word *racism* lost its abrasive power somewhere in the Nixon era, cynicism still has no defenders. Doubt, pessimism—those things are downright un-American. But beneath the word game, Obama was asking one portion of the country to slough off two centuries of its history and asking another to believe that the first was willing and capable of doing so.

All politicians need large enemies against which to define themselves: The usual suspects include "the lobbyists," "the special interests," "the media," and the nameless, greed-infected CEOs. Obama took occasional aim at those targets but also waged war against a national mood, a jaded disposition. For eight disastrous years the American economy had been pushed to ruin and vengeance had become a substitute for foreign policy, so this strategy was understandable. As he sought the confidence of millions of skeptical voters who could not pronounce or spell his name at first, battling cynicism made sense. But what went unstated and nearly unnoticed was that in battling cynicism, he was challenging black voters as much as white ones. He was asking black America to step away from its own perspective of history and believe that a black man could become president. That required both audacity and vast reserves of hope.

Certain cynical luxuries come with being black in this country, like the ability to shrug off the dime-store rites of patriotism. We've generally seen America through a perpetually raised eyebrow, a *yeah, whatever* perspective that comes with the terrain on this side of American history. This is not fatalism, the belief that change is impossible. Rather, it is the knowledge that for every bit of it you achieve, you will pay a premium plus interest.

Older folk reserve the term *backsliding* for those Christians who understand the righteous path but habitually wander back into the thickets of sin. American history is one of democratic backsliding. In 1865, just after the Thirteenth Amendment formally ended slavery, friends of Frederick Douglass approached him about disbanding the old antislavery societies. Douglass advised them that it would be unwise to do so. Slavery was no more, but "we must see what new shape this old snake will take next." His warning proved prescient: In place of slavery came the bitter regime of sharecropping and the terrorism of the Ku Klux Klan. Lynching revoked freedom. Decades later, on the verge of the first world war, W. E. B. Du Bois urged blacks to close ranks with the nation and fight in the war, even in a segregated army; he believed their patriotism would yield a freedom dividend at home. Instead, black soldiers upon their return were lynched in uniform.

The ghosts of Memphis haunt us still. The disbelief in progress is tied to the image of Martin Luther King Jr., sprawled on a balcony at the Lorraine Motel. And that of Malcolm X at the Audubon Ballroom. And Medgar Evers's blood-ruined driveway in Mississippi. And any of the nameless catalogue of casualties, men and women guilty only of taking the Constitution at face value.

The fruits of this history were visible in the initial reaction of many African Americans to Barack Obama's candidacy. A year before the inauguration I walked the streets of Denmark, South Carolina, knocking on doors and handing out Obama campaign materials. In those days Hillary Clinton held a significant national advantage over Obama among black voters. They held her husband in high regard; she had greater name recognition and massive financial advantages. Time and again I encountered people who believed they were doing Obama a favor by not supporting him. "He has two small children," they would point out. "He needs to be around to see them grow up." Or "I want to support him; I just don't know what might happen . . . ," and the sentence would trail off, leaving bad echoes of the past to fill in the blanks.

In asking for their vote, Obama was necessarily asking people to part with this inheritance of doubt. In February 2007 the Obamas sat down for an interview with *60 Minutes*. Steve Kroft delicately asked Michelle Obama whether she feared for her husband's life. Her reply was, "As a black man, Barack could be shot going to the gas station." This was a statement that could have been comforting only to black people. At that crucial moment she decided to be optimistic, albeit in the most cynical way possible. The possibility of violent death is truly a bitter, unspoken reality for black men in this country. Black males are nearly ten times more likely than their white peers to be victims of homicide. Michelle Obama was born and raised in Chicago, and her statement reflected a certain South Side pragmatism: If going to the store means taking your life in your hands, why *wouldn't* you run for president? It was simply a matter of relative risks. Four of forty-three presidents had died violently. The stats for a black man who resides on the South Side of Chicago might be roughly comparable. In either case, her response put a different spin on the issue of his safety.[1]

In January 2008 Caroline Kennedy endorsed Barack Obama for president. Like many people that year, she reported that her children had convinced her to support his candidacy. A common storyline of the election was that younger Americans identified with the cool candidate, regardless of his race, and convinced their parents to vote for him. In black America that story had a particular twist: The younger generation convinced the older one not only that he could win but that he could be safe. This was the hidden implication of Obama's theme "Change you can believe in"—it meant different things to different people. For one portion of the public, it meant that a nation could change its path, reaffirm its commitment to democracy, and meet titanic challenges. For another, it meant that a man could step outside the rules of history and live to tell about it.

This battered belief in progress—however fragmented and however great the costs—is the most fundamentally American aspect of the black experience. But the ligament of hope was not enough to support the idea of a black president. Prior to his entry into the election, only a handful of African Americans believed that Barack Obama could win—and all of them lived at the same address on the South Side of Chicago. In the face of history, their doubt was more akin to realism than cynicism. Between 1876 and 2008 a grand total of three black people had been elected to the U.S. Senate. Only two had served as governor. The most powerful African Americans—Thurgood Marshall, Colin Powell, Condoleezza Rice, Clarence Thomas—gained their positions through political appointments, a testament to the influence of their white patrons but certainly not evidence of an ability to actually win elections.

For these reasons the road to black support ran through a state with a 94 percent white population. Victory in the Iowa caucuses was a necessity, the closing argument in Obama's case to black America. I viewed the Iowa returns at a watch party on the northwest side of Atlanta. State senators and city council reps politicked around the floor. Reverend Joseph Lowery, the civil rights icon and former lieutenant to Martin Luther King Jr., sat on the far side of the room; local pols pooled around him, trying, it seemed, to gain endorsement by proximity. When Obama was announced as the winner of the caucuses, the party roared. But what struck me was the look of shock on the face of an older black man near me. His jaw literally hung open, and he stared at the screen for long, speechless moments, his hat askew. He was seeing something, a version of America, maybe, that he had never expected to witness.

Long after the restaurant closed, small clusters of people, mostly black, huddled in the frigid parking lot, talking about the meaning of what they had just seen. Like Joe Louis during the Jim Crow days, it struck me, a single individual had offered a new definition of heroism; talent and circumstance had elevated one person to become a surrogate for millions of others. That night stood out for another reason: It was the first time I saw an Obama T-shirt with a picture of the candidate. Not long before the final tally, a large, middle-aged white man came in wearing a shirt that said: HE'S BLACK, I'M PROUD.

Such scenes, repeated in small gatherings, campaign offices, and random conversations, opened doors. After the caucuses Lowery explained, "Black folk have already had a symbolic candidate with Jesse in 1988, and they did not want to throw away a vote on more symbolism. Barack Obama had to prove that he could actually win white votes before he could count on black ones." The following week a small army of volunteers left Atlanta for South Carolina. Just before the primary, the Atlanta offices were sending campaign workers into the state twenty-five vans at a time.[2]

In many ways Obama was swimming against the tide of tradition, but in other ways he had history on his side. Synchronized dates made it appear that he had a kind of spiritual momentum: He was campaigning for the presidency forty years after the assassination of Martin Luther King. As the weeks passed, the two men were increasingly paired in street vendor iconography. Outside one campaign office I saw a man wearing a shirt with the image of both men and the caption THE DREAMER AND THE DREAM. The children of Israel wandered for forty years before entering the Promised Land—this biblical metaphor was added to Obama's growing résumé of symbolism. Those confluences followed him throughout the year. His nomination took place on August 28, 2008, the forty-fifth anniversary of the March on Washington (and lamentably the fifty-third anniversary of Emmett Till's lynching). John Lewis, the sole living speaker from the 1963 March on Washington, was now a congressman who, after some prodding, endorsed Obama and spoke at the nomination. And Obama's 2009 inauguration took place the day after the observance of the Martin Luther King Jr. holiday. Thus in placing his hand on Lincoln's

Bible, he had not simply been inaugurated as the president of the United States; on some level, he also became a barometer of history.

Historians will spend years deciphering the subtle changes in American society that led to Obama's election. Just after he won, people commonly credited George W. Bush with paving the way for the nation's first black president. Two wars, a sunken economy, and fallen national prestige were just part of the picture. So were the superior organization, elocution, and fund-raising genius of both the candidate and the team. The truth is that none of us really know how it happened. But the more compelling question is why Obama thought it possible in the first place. In a season in which historic developments seemed to occur almost weekly, the first and possibly greatest accomplishment of Obama and his team was their recognition that the political climate offered a path to victory.

"They said this day would never come." Obama began his victory speech in Iowa with those words. It was a gentleman's version of "I told you so," informing the country that it had changed in ways that it had not even imagined. After the New Hampshire primary he rallied his dejected supporters with the mantra "Yes, we can"—another shot at the cynics. And so the hope assault went for twenty-two months, until the final landing at Grant Park and "Change has come to America."

In the midst of national celebration, pointing out the old continuities seemed nearly blasphemous. We do violence to distill the moment down solely to race, but race was nonetheless the active ingredient in that democratic bliss. And it remains crucial to understanding this moment that we recognize that black advances have generally come at the behest of some larger imperative. Slavery ended as a consequence not just of the Civil War but of the fact that the Union was *losing* the Civil War. Lincoln's gesture of emancipation suited the needs of more whites than blacks—some twenty million Northerners ultimately relied upon those ex-slaves to join the fight against the Confederacy and preserve their cherished Union.

The civil rights movement occurred in the context of the Cold War, at a point when racism had become an international liability. Jim Crow could be ignored when it was simply a domestic concern, but once it became an embarrassment in world affairs, its demise was swift. Here is a basic truth: People are driven by self-interest. But America has an overwhelming need to dress self-interest in the finery of moral conviction.

Great acts of individual conscience were performed in the 1860s and in the 1960s, but absent some bigger incentive, they would have remained just that. Ultimately the gears of morality had to be greased by self-interest. Obama, more than most, understands this dynamic. As a community organizer, he began with the premise that people are driven by self-interest, and he understood that that is key to creating social change.

Obama's election stands out in part because it did not come in the context of violence. No war, no images of bloodied idealists beaten in the streets, gave rise to it. Some felt that perhaps history was the down payment, that we had accumulated enough blood equity to pay for it in advance. But even the moment of democratic bliss remained part of the old pattern: It was in the national self-interest to move away from the abomination of the Bush–Bin Laden era. The nation had the wisdom, insight, and yes, self-interest to elect a man whose middle name is Hussein, and who had been partly raised in Indonesia, an Islamic country. His vast talents and brown skin would mark a moral transition so vast that his election would appear entirely and objectively as an act of goodwill and good faith.

Toward the end of the general election campaign, the blogger and statistician Nate Silver relayed an anecdote that stood out even amid the tsunami of electoral details that had become a feature of daily life. A campaign worker, a white man canvassing for Barack Obama, knocked on the door of a white family in rural Pennsylvania. A woman answered the door. He asked her if she knew who she was voting for, and she replied without a trace of irony, "We're voting for the nigger." He initially suspected that this was her way of stiff-arming campaign workers, who were perceived in a category somewhere between locusts and telemarketers. Then she relayed the question to her husband, who shouted from the back of the house, "Yeah, we're voting for the nigger." Considered in isolation, this incident would be one of those idiosyncratic moments that people puzzle over briefly before moving on. But I heard similar stories from journalists, organizers, and random political folk. In another version, a reporter interviewed a white couple just outside Atlanta who confessed: "I know he's a nigger, but I just don't trust McCain on the economy."[3]

It was ugly progress, an off-brand version of "change you could believe in." Richard Nixon won the presidency in 1968 by remembering a principle as old as the Republic: Racial resentment can persuade whites to ignore their own economic interests. In 1980 Ronald Reagan recognized that Nixon's Southern Strategy could work in the rest of the country. Economically marginal Southern whites were more willing to endorse the laissez faire, antiunion politics of the GOP if it meant that they stood a chance to halt the advance march of civil rights. Labor union members did vote for the staunchly antiunion Reagan, because he would keep the welfare queens in check. Only in America do we find a factory worker and the CEO who just fired him supporting the same presidential candidate. During the 2008 primary season the media served warmed-over helpings of this principle: the West Virginia voter who claimed that Barack Obama wanted to enslave whites; the Texas Democrat who swore he would vote for McCain if the black guy got the nomination; the Clinton supporters who vowed to stay home if she weren't the nominee.

Other presumptions went stale that year too. Reams of data show that tough economic times lead to increased racial animosity. During the Great Depression white men gathered in street-corner mobs demanding that there be "no work for niggers" until every white man had a job. The social goodwill of the civil rights era evaporated amid the economic hardships of the 1970s. For those of us who know this history, its repetition is a given. At least it was until recently. Two months before the election, the bottom fell out of the stock market. John McCain theatrically suspended his campaign and rushed to Washington to address the financial crisis, but his numbers went south anyway. Another old truth was falling away. Despite tough economic times, Barack Obama won 53 percent of the vote and a larger portion of the white vote than any previous Democrat since Lyndon B. Johnson, larger than Bill Clinton, whose two terms were greatly aided by Ross Perot pulling votes from the first president Bush and then from Bob Dole.

At some point in 2008 people concluded that race was simply not a luxury they could afford to keep in the foreground, not with unemployment rising and a Republican nominee who admittedly knew little about economics. In the end, the story of 2008 is not diminished because it was driven by self-interest. Rather, it is enhanced by the fact that people were mature enough to recognize what their self-interests were.

In the opening pages of *The Audacity of Hope*, Obama declared, "I am new enough on the national political scene that I serve as a blank screen on which people of vastly different political stripes project their own views. As such, I am bound to disappoint some, if not all, of them."[4] But his symbolism was derived from his identity, not from his novelty. The black congressman Harold Ford was new to the public when he delivered the keynote speech to the 2000 Democratic National Convention, but no one ever accused him of standing in the tide of history or embodying our dreams.

Obama's identity was knotted and tangled with global currents of freedom and colonialism; it also had direct implications domestically. In America the prohibitions against racial mixture are literally older than the nation itself. In 1630 a white man named Hugh Davis was publicly whipped for fouling himself and for "dishonoring God" by his fornication with a Negro woman. In 1662 Virginia authored laws forbidding interracial sex and ensuring that the child of any such union would follow the status of the mother—a quiet wink directed to white men taking liberties with enslaved black women. In 1691 Virginia outlawed marriage between black and white residents altogether. Out of this fixation on purity and categories grew the lore of the tragic mulatto, a sort of cultural keep-out sign warning both races of the disastrous consequences of mingling. The very term *mulatto* derived from the word *mule*: the product of dissimilar species.

For centuries lore, then fiction, then film remixed this story-line, all with the common theme that the product of these unions could come to no good end. But during the course of the election campaign, Obama consistently turned this body of myths inside out. The deployment of his white family members in commercials was a not-so-subtle reversal of the one-drop rule that deemed that if you were black at all, you were all black. But even as Obama identified himself as a black man, he could—whether intentionally or not—appeal to white voters as not entirely different from them. At the Denver convention John Kerry would ask the audience to recognize Obama's uncle, who had fought in World War II, and the camera would pan to an aged white man who would not have been out of place at the local VFW hall. The black delegates in the hall roared as if Obama had just played an inside joke, and on some level he had. One remarked, "If I had a white uncle, I'd take him to every job interview I ever went to."

Understandably this emphasis generated claims that the candidate should be thought of as biracial, not as black. But those claims missed the point entirely. Obama is technically biracial, but only corkscrew logic holds that the rest of black America isn't as well. To insist that Obama be designated only half black is to somehow presume that half is greater than four eighths or sixteen thirty-seconds or any of the other geometrics of race hidden in our family trees. By most estimates well over 90 percent of those deemed African American are of mixed white (and frequently Native American) ancestry. Black America is a racial amalgamation that has adopted the most convenient, least confusing terminology for itself: black.

Declaring that Barack Obama was not black necessarily

meant arguing that there was no such thing as black America and that America had nearly no black people. It meant the retroactive removal of Frederick Douglass, W. E. B. Du Bois, Bob Marley, Booker T. Washington, Malcolm X, and Adam Clayton Powell from the roster of black achievers, as all had known white ancestry. Obama was as black as any of the 36 million people laboring, living, working, struggling, and flourishing in America under that designation. Barack Obama is, in fact, biracial. But then, so is Michelle.

These are the subthemes; they tend to be lost beneath the numbers. In the final tally of 2008 Obama won 97 percent of the black vote. Blacks between eighteen and twenty-nine had the highest voter turnout of any group, and 69 percent of black women voted—a higher percentage than white women or men of any race. I suspect that these voters were not high on symbolism and based their vote on more sober considerations. His clever deployments of black English and Malcolm X quotes would have come to naught if people had not believed in his agenda and capacity for leadership. The identity simply ensured that those people would find themselves choked up in the voting booth. Barack Obama also won a higher percentage of white voters than did John Kerry, Al Gore, or Bill Clinton in 1992 or 1996. His symbolic value to these voters can't be ignored, but they were not intoxicated by symbolism either. A needless war and a fractured economy for once trumped the fault lines of race. Yet only one of these storylines echoed across the media.

On November 5, 2008, the *New York Times* noted that a historic barrier had fallen, but it missed another story worthy of a headline: Obama had asked black America to judge him by the content of his character, not by the color of his skin—and had gotten their votes anyway.

CHAPTER 2

Of Jeremiah Wright

THE MEANING OF CHANGE ON THE SOUTH SIDE OF AMERICA

IN ONE WAY or another Barack Obama's identity was at the center of most of the questions surrounding his politics. That was why his Republican rivals consistently returned to the theme "Who is Barack Obama?" To the extent that politicians write books, they are usually about policy or what's wrong with Washington. Obama had authored a four-hundred-page tome explaining, quite simply, who he was and how he came to be that person.

We are accustomed to politicians coming with their own shorthand: war hero, solid midwesterner, business leader. George W. Bush styled himself a cowboy and bought a ranch shortly before his presidential campaign to prove it. But someone like Obama had no shorthand, which was both a problem and an opportunity. He acknowledged as much in *The Audacity of Hope* when he wrote: "I am a prisoner of my own biography: I can't help but view the American experience through the lens of a black man of mixed heritage, forever mindful of how generations of people who looked like me were subjugated and stigmatized, and the subtle and not so subtle ways that race and class continue to shape our lives." But if biography was a prison, it was also a source of liberation. During the campaign fringe groups argued that Obama was not an American citizen. Ridiculous as that claim was, it highlights an important reality: Although Obama was born an American citizen, on many levels he views America through the eyes of an immigrant.

As a child, Obama spent four years in Indonesia. In his memoir he details the slow descent of his stepfather from a young idealist into a dull-hearted bureaucrat, a man resigned to the crooked tilt of the world he inhabits. When tax officials visit, the family must hide their refrigerator in a storage room. Students who have studied abroad are distrusted by the government and subject to random imprisonment, or they simply, ominously disappear. Obama's own father fell from grace in Kenya, his life the bitter parable of a Harvard-educated economics minister who ran afoul of the president and suffered ruin for it. Barack Obama Sr. was a member of the minority Luo ethnicity, and even before his clash with the president, his ancestry placed a ceiling on his potential in Kenyan politics. In Obama's telling, neither man found anything uncommon in his fate: bitter and difficult but not unusual, the way of the world.

The most common theme in Obama's campaign speeches, besides hope and change, was the idea of fairness, of a one-to-one relationship between effort and opportunity. This is partly political boilerplate, but Obama was also speaking from the heart. At one point during the debates he mentioned that Americans who want to start a small business or apply for a driver's license do not expect to pay a bribe.

American citizens take this situation for granted—at least, those who were born and raised entirely in this country do. But it immediately stands out to an immigrant. A portion of American history is rendered in deep sepia, the story of the huddled masses crowded into Ellis Island seeking freedom. The story was always more complex than that, but it was nonetheless the version that the country liked to put before the world. That streets-of-gold myth expired long ago, but for good or nil Obama's election gave it a renewed credibility.

These things are worth considering. In India the Dalit have been shackled to the bottom of society for fourteen hundred years. In the Muslim world the battles between Sunni and Shia have raged for more than a millennium, and in eastern Europe the Roma have been an exploited class for more than six centuries. In the United States 144 years separate the slave from the president. For Ann Nixon Cooper, the 106-year-old Atlantan who voted for Barack Obama, that transition took place inside a single generation: Her parents were slaves.

Argentina, Great Britain, India, Israel, Liberia, and Pakistan have all elected women as heads of state, but no industrial nation has elected to leadership a member of its minority class. Not only is Obama black in a way that we've scarcely seen before, he is *American* in ways we've hardly considered. The simple combination of his pigment and the presidential seal of the United States speaks volumes about the American creed of social mobility to the rest of the world.

In late February 2008 Obama rattled off eleven consecutive primary victories—what some sardonically called the Black History Month Massacre—and people began to take seriously the notion that he might actually become president. Somewhere during those weeks I wondered if millions of whites would have voted for him if he had grown up in a black family on the South Side of Chicago rather than a white one in Hawaii and Indonesia. His paeans to opportunity and fairness were not the lines that resonated most with black voters. As he sang the country's praises at the 2004 convention, one woman openly rolled her eyes. But that was also part of his immigrant perspective. He spoke of that distinction in *Dreams from My Father*:

> Power . . . In America it generally remained hidden from view until you dug beneath the surface of things; until you visited an Indian reservation or spoke to a black person whose trust you had earned. But here [in Indonesia] power was undisguised, indiscriminate, naked, always fresh in the memory.[5]

Regardless of Obama's eventual standing as a paragon of black history, at the outset African Americans didn't know quite what to do with him. His experiences allowed him to understand blackness in ways that were different from African Americans who grew up in this country. The obstacles of race in America are one thing; the obstacles of corrupt and arbitrary national power are something else entirely. The Jamaican-born writer Joan Morgan observes that for all the useless early debates over whether Obama was "really" an African American, his experience more closely echoed that of Caribbean immigrants than that of native-born American blacks. On one level this remark is an instance of the kaleidoscope effect, the way vastly different people could look at Obama and see something of themselves reflected back at them. But her point has something to it. "We're not shackled to a pessimistic view of what America can be," she told me. "We come from places where the economic conditions are often much worse, where there may not be access to running water. We arrive with this idea that if you work hard you can do well."[6]

In 2004 the *New York Times* reported that as much as two thirds of the black student population at Harvard was either immigrant, children of immigrants, or biracial, leading one administrator to comment that it was a reflection of Horatio Alger, not *Brown v. Board*. Children of black immigrants outperform native-descended blacks academically and economically—just as many other immigrant groups outperform American whites. The difference is the relative faith in possibility. Obama's biography placed him in a position to simultaneously see the obstacle of race and the possibilities of America.[7]

THE BLACK MAN who became president rose to national prominence in 2004 on the grace of a speech in which he declared, *"There is not a black America or a white America . . . there is the United States of America."* That is already the most italic-worthy sentence of this young century. But it is also untrue. We

desperately want it to be true, and more than any other politician of our era, Barack Obama is the beneficiary of a vision that
we believe in but that does not exist. At least not yet. And certainly not at the time he gave the speech.

Here is what we know of the various Americas on that night
in August 2004. Some 21 percent of black men in their twenties
were incarcerated, and one third of black children were living in
poverty. Hispanics were 3.3 times more likely to be in prison
than whites, and their per capita income was 50 percent of their
white counterparts. Some 35.9 million Americans—more than
10 percent of the total population—lived below the poverty line,
and the quality of public education reflected those disparities.
There was not only a black America and a white America, but a
rich one and a poor one, a privileged one and a neglected one,
an America where much was possible and one anchored in place
by despair.

Viewed through the lens of history, those seventeen words
created new realities—immediately for Obama, and eventually
for the rest of us. When Franklin Roosevelt said there was nothing to fear but fear itself, he was not being truthful or was
at least vastly understating the matter. The American masses,
the dispossessed and foreclosed veterans of the Dust Bowl and
the breadline, knew this, but they appreciated the underlying
sentiment—that for this man hard times could not slay idealism.
Similarly, in telling his own untruth, Barack Obama was adver-
tising himself as an American daring enough to discard history,
or at least to diminish its authority over the present.

Nations are narrations. They rely upon creation myths to
explain their character, much as Genesis prepares us to understand the Old Testament God. The American creation myth is
the story of thirteen colonies led by a band of patriots who
rose up to defeat an empire. The men who led this revolt sought
to divorce history. They had surveyed their surroundings and
seen enough of bloodlines and titles, of power inherited by the
corrupt and bequeathed to the inept. Their pyramid-shaped

world was governed by a fistful of pedigreed nobles and the god-sanctioned tyrants they served. The Founders offered an alternative vision, one in which leaders drew their authority from people, not from gods, and where intelligence and skill were the criteria for government, not the murky will of a supreme being. Their revolution, we understand, was not driven by taxes and tea; it was a struggle to pry away the cold fingers of tradition and to retire ideas that were beyond their expiration date.

But step outside the grand myths, and other truths become self-evident. In a cold-eyed parallel version of the story, we see Jefferson denounce the slave trade in the first Declaration of Independence, only to delete that sentence and edit black freedom out of existence. We see enslaved hands build the White House and the U.S. Capitol. Freedom, when it comes, requires four years of war and six hundred thousand deaths, but the emancipation is brittle, as weak as it is temporary. Jump forward a half century, and we see women boarding a ship to sail to France. They are going to visit the graves of their sons who fell in battle and were buried there during World War I. Black soldiers died to Make the World Safe for Democracy, but their mothers travel at the bottom of those ships, because equality is not permitted, not even in grief.

This alternate story tells us there are blood traditions rooted deep in American soil, that none of us is ever truly ahead of our time, and that history does not relinquish its claims easily. The Founders did not destroy the old pyramid; they simply turned it upside down. In place of a world where the masses were ruled by a tiny minority, they built one where only a minority was powerless. They substituted an aristocracy of skin tones for the aristocracy of blood lines.

There is more than one storyline and therefore more than one America. In 1852 Frederick Douglass asked a question that has echoed down through generations, each finding a new answer, a question that Barack Obama's election forces us to revisit.

"What to the American slave is your 4th of July?" Douglass asked. His own reply was a bile-filled indictment:

> I answer; a day that reveals to him, more than all other days in the year, the gross injustice and cruelty to which he is the constant victim. To him, your celebration is a sham; your boasted liberty, an unholy license; your national greatness, swelling vanity; your sounds of rejoicing are empty and heartless; your denunciation of tyrants brass fronted impudence; your shout of liberty and equality, hollow mockery; your prayers and hymns, your sermons and thanks-givings, with all your religious parade and solemnity, are to him, mere bombast, fraud, deception, impiety, and hypocrisy—a thin veil to cover up crimes which would disgrace a nation of savages.[8]

There stands the contradiction. Douglass's question haunts through history like a Freudian nightmare, destined to recur until the underlying conflict is resolved. Five years after he asked it, the U.S. Supreme Court took it up indirectly. Writing the majority opinion in the case of *Dred Scott v. Sandford*, Chief Justice Roger Taney deduced that the words *Negro* and *citizen* were mutually exclusive. The Negro, in his telling, had no rights that a white man was bound to respect: "It is too clear for dispute, that the enslaved African race were not intended to be included, and formed no part of the people who framed and adopted this Declaration [of Independence]." In 1896 Homer Adolph Plessy sought to overturn Louisiana's segregation laws, resurrecting the issue, and the high court halved the nation with "separate but equal."

In 1903 W. E. B. Du Bois, in his visionary *Souls of Black Folk*, explained to the world:

> One ever feels his twoness—an American, a Negro; two souls, two thoughts, two unreconciled strivings; two warring ideals in one dark body, whose dogged strength alone keeps it from being torn asunder.

In March 1968 the question recurred in the Kerner Commission's *Report on Civil Disorders*. In the wake of four consecutive summers of racial violence, Lyndon B. Johnson's advisory committee wrote: "Our nation is moving toward two societies, one black, one white, separate and unequal." A month later Martin Luther King Jr. was assassinated, inaugurating yet more days of fire and chaos.

In the intervening years irregular flashpoints have defined us: the low-grade fever of culture wars; the hypertensive debates over affirmative action and welfare; the Rodney King riots; the serial race saga of O. J. Simpson; the brutality visited upon Abner Louima and Amadou Diallo and Oscar Grant. All reminded us that history is not yet in the past.

In stark contrast to this storyline came Barack Obama's words: "There is not a black America or a white America, . . . there is the United States of America." The statement was either a denial or a prophecy, but it was certainly generous. On some level the absolution was an old trick. At the turn of the twentieth century Booker T. Washington became the most powerful black man in America on the strength of a speech in which he made common cause with segregation: "In all things social we can be separate as the fingers, yet one as the hand in all things essential to mutual progress." At the precise point where the cast of separation was hardening, Washington described it as doing just the opposite. (Emancipation robbed him of the chance to charge "There is not a slave America or a free America . . .") It has been said that Barack Obama wrote his way into the presidency. At the crucial junctures in his campaign, he opted to speak to the country as if we were a nation of rational adults. The speech to the Boston Democratic Convention in 2004 stands at least slightly outside that stream. He was not making his peace with anything as onerous as Jim Crow; rather, he was offering a redacted version of the national condition.

Dial back to that moment, and you begin to notice small themes that imprinted themselves. Over the next four years the arc and structure of his speeches became recognizable—the balance of poetry and policy, using his unique biography as an advantage, offering the panoramic view of a complex problem, arguing that we have been mired in false dichotomies in approaching this one, and then offering a commonsense, pragmatic, nonideological alternative spiced with just enough idealism to spark the imagination of young people. This pattern was still a novelty when he strode onto the stage at the Fleet Center. He had not yet gone iconic: The suit was cut too broad in the shoulders, with a surplus in the lapels; he was still captive to his own formality and remove— traits he would soon shed. Observing the speech at the time, I wrote that "by the standards of black oratory the speech heard around the world was a B-plus" and argued that Jesse Jackson's incandescent address to the 1988 convention remained the standard by which speeches should be judged. But I also recognized that something beyond the form was at play.

Standing in Boston that night, Obama had the political wisdom to deliver a feature, not a documentary; a vision of what the country might become, not a report on what it was at that moment. The magnanimity of that act might go unappreciated until you think about it this way: Here was a black man standing at the midway point of a disastrous presidency and offering the country a plot twist, a balm for both its bitter history and its present despair. It was philanthropy for Americans' bankrupt morale, really. "We are one people, all of us pledging allegiance to the United States." He spoke those words with earnest fervor. Understood from that angle, he could almost reasonably be seen, in the eyes of many, as a candidate for the presidency.

In the long term this way of looking at America through its best tendencies was possibly Barack Obama's greatest political asset. In the short term, however, his differences with his former pastor Jeremiah Wright lay at the heart of his most bitter and complicated political crisis.

REVEREND JEREMIAH WRIGHT lives in one version of America, the one located on the South Side of Chicago and rooted in hard memory and fractured promises. Obama is also a product of Chicago. As president, he channels the city in the way that Johnson could only have come from Texas or Kennedy from Boston. True, Obama is not from Chicago originally, but that somehow makes the city even more central to his storyline.

Dreams from My Father relays the tale of a biracial world-wanderer searching for a fixed answer to the question of identity. Obama found it among the seven hundred thousand black people living, striving, and struggling on the city's South Side. Although his outward appearance was indistinguishable from that of any other black person in America, he had never had sustained contact with any black institution. His interactions and early friendships with black peers read like a series of morality tales, each individual adding to the questions beneath the surface. He found a home in a place that had been defined and redefined by the tides of migration for a century. Understanding Obama and his relationship to Jeremiah Wright and the Trinity United Church of Christ, almost certainly requires an understanding of what Chicago symbolized to those Negro legions pouring into it from points south. It requires an understanding of the South Side of the city and by extension the south sides of cities across America that were being shaped by similar forces.

In the early twentieth century the South Side of Chicago began as a depot for migrant aspirations. Hostile legislation and the onset of the first world war dammed the flow of European immigrants into the United States and opened up new opportunities for American Negroes. The nation's rail lines became arteries leading out of the Jim Crow world and into the new industrial one.

Their migration was no passive act—wind-blown people tumbling along the tides of history—but deliberate motion. Robert Sengstacke Abbott's *Chicago Defender* newspaper urged Negroes to abandon the dead-end options at home—tearing up sod in the hope God would grant a few nickels' worth of cotton, perpetual debt, tending the babies of those who made you live on your knees—and come north to a new promised land.

Between 1910 and 1940 nearly two million black people left the rural South, many of whom found their way to the Windy City. And if its promises weren't kept, a fragment of hope could be found in the fact that people at least felt obliged to make them.

The cities consumed their labor and corralled them into the neglected precincts. Bronzeville. Harlem. The Hill District. The same story was replayed on the streets of Philadelphia and Boston and Gary and Detroit: Negroes came north in locust numbers that meant overcrowded housing, classrooms swollen beyond capacity, and competition for scarce resources. But their numbers also began to change the nature of their world. And they meant power. In Brooklyn, Branch Rickey decided to integrate the Dodgers partly because it was right but largely to give thousands of black Brooklynites an incentive to visit Ebbets Field. In Chicago a black congressman could be elected in 1928 and then be succeeded by another black candidate in 1934. The storyline grew vastly more complex: Rural poverty gave way to the opaque possibilities of slum life in the places where Richard Wright, Gwendolyn Brooks, and Gordon Parks brought their brilliant work to fruition.

This is the world that Jeremiah Wright represented. Long before Obama's journey to the White House began, Wright was a Philadelphia-born seminary student at the University of Chicago, a product of historically black Howard University. He was also a member of Omega Psi Phi, the black fraternity that prides itself on audacious nonconformity and whose members include Jesse Jackson, Michael Jordan, and Vernon Jordan. At age thirty-one he became pastor of Trinity United Methodist Church, a small institution on the South Side with a couple hundred members. As a pastor he occupied a niche that was part alderman, part counselor, part supervisor, and part economic adviser. In *Dreams from My Father* Obama recounts his first encounter with Wright, as an outgrowth of his community organizing work on the South Side. The facile connection was that Obama found a father figure in the older man, but there was something broader at work as well. A black man whose life had been untouched by any black institution entered into dialogue with a man who was nearly the embodiment of one.

James Baldwin once observed:

> The Black preacher, since the church was the only Civilized instition that we were permitted—separately—to enter, was our first warrior, *terrorist*, or *guerrilla. He* said that freedom was real—that *we* were real. *He* told us that *trouble don't last always. He* told us that our children and elders were sacred, when the Civilized were spitting on them and hacking them to pieces, in the name of God, and in order to keep on making money.[9]

Though later observers would have no problem associating Wright with the word *terrorist*, they largely overlooked the fact that he does not exist in a vacuum. The black clergy are part of a prophetic tradition that seeks to leverage the moral authority of God toward the aims of social justice. Largely unconcerned with offending the sensibilities of larger society, they are quick to remind you that Nat Turner was a clergyman. Jeremiah Wright's role, on one level, was to conjure storms and break down walls like his biblical namesake. The black church began with slaves seeking a place to speak their own unsanctioned truths—controversy was practically part of the pastor's job description. Naturally this mandate to shout down injustice would primarily focus on racial themes; it was the most obvious and consistent form of injustice in the community's daily experience.

Prior to the turbulent spring of 2008, Wright was a highly regarded and fairly uncontroversial figure in and beyond the circles of black clergy. His name was primarily connected to the massive church that he had built during his three decades in the pulpit. Others knew of his outspoken condemnation of the apartheid regime in South Africa and his advocacy for community causes. A few would smirkingly mention his habit of occasionally cussing in the pulpit, but nearly all regarded him as someone who would say things that needed to be said. His skill in the pulpit was such that when jazz critic Stanley Crouch wanted someone to preach "Premature Autopsy for a Noble Art Form," his metaphoric eulogy for the blues, he turned to Wright. By midspring all this was so much white noise.

The media exists not so much to clarify misunderstandings as to ensure that debate continues. Wright likely overlooked this curious, built-in conflict of interest, but Obama's campaign was intensely aware of it. An early harbinger came when *New York Times* reporter Jodi Kantor wrote an article about Obama's spiritual journey. Wright, who had been interviewed, disagreed with the content of the article and penned an indignant letter to the reporter. Full of flourishes and erudition, it was nonetheless the letter of a man unaccustomed to handling national media.

> Out of a two-hour conversation with you about Barack's spiritual journey and my protesting to you that I had not shaped him nor formed him, that I had not mentored him or made him the man he was, even though I would love to take that credit, you did not print any of that . . . out of two hours of conversation I spent approximately five to seven minutes on Barack's taking advice from one of his trusted campaign people and deeming it unwise to make me the media spotlight on the day of his announcing his candidacy for the Presidency and what do you print? You and your editor proceeded to present to the general public a snippet, a printed "sound byte" and a titillating and tantalizing article about his disinviting me to the Invocation on the day of his announcing his candidacy.[10]

He concluded by telling Kantor that she would do well at the paper, as the *New York Times* had no integrity.

In his initial foray Obama pointed out that Wright was "just his pastor." But that didn't quite square: In many quarters of the black community, the word *just* is incapable of modifying the phrase *my pastor*—the clergy hold too much authority. It would be akin to saying someone is "just my defense attorney" or "only my heart surgeon." This was certainly the case for a figure as revered and influential as Jeremiah Wright.

Charisma does many things for those blessed to possess it, but it serves primarily as camouflage. Muhammad Ali was a charmed harlequin who made his living punching people in the face, yet somehow people never thought of him as particularly *violent* or *mean*. His mode of performance exacerbated that effect; he didn't so much throw punches as lash his long arms out, a gloved fist snapping at the end of a whip. It did not look like he was hurting his opponent, but the cumulative effect was devastating.

To the close observer, the 2008 campaign revealed something of Ali in Obama's political style. Obama might have simply been an earnest community organizer who found Jesus, but he was also aware—or soon became aware—of Trinity's virtues as a political base. Wright was portal as much as pastor, and even if joining the church was not a mercenary act on Obama's part, gaining Wright's help was a visible fringe benefit.

How then does this lead us to *"Goddamn America, Goddamn America, Goddamn America, Goddamn America . . ."*?

In response to the charge that they were going easy on the Illinois senator, the media began excavating Wright's old sermons. A bit of digital archaeology unearthed a six-year-old speech that Jeremiah Wright had given in response to 9/11. The most toxic excerpts represented a minuscule fraction of his body of writings, but that didn't matter much. What did matter was that presidential campaigns have been derailed for far less than association with a man who spat condemnation at the flag. Gary Hart's ambitions were a casualty of routine beltway bedhopping. In 1972 Edmund Muskie was guilty only of getting choked up on the campaign trail, but that was enough to send his poll numbers tanking. And Howard Dean's 2004 hopes turned flammable because of a single off-key shout. By comparison, Obama's Jeremiah Wright problem was thermonuclear. The speech Obama gave, the most crucial of his career to that point, was campaign triage.

By any standard, the "race speech," as it came to be known, was a work of brilliance. In an era where politicians routinely farm out political speeches like piecework to teams of writers and then cobble them into a whole, Obama composed a single, cohesive observation of an American circumstance. He seeded this speech with aspects of his own biography—the biracial lineage, the globe-flung family ties. If the national creed was "Out of many, one," here was a candidate whose kaleidoscopic history stated "Out of one, many." He had never set out to be "the black candidate"—he was running for president of the USA, not of BET. The point of the speech was to somehow address race—even under duress—without being defined by it. The thoughtfulness and insight, the fluid stream of logic, stood far outside the standard fare of political oratory. It was the first but far from the final time that he used his background as a college professor to his advantage. Conservative critics—Juan Williams chief among them—were left to quibble that his comparison of Wright's statements to racially obtuse commentary from his grandmother was a case of false equivalence. No matter. The speech contained other actual moments of false equivalence—his allusions to the segregation-inspired racial bitterness in black communities and the belief among whites that they had been denied fair opportunity by affirmative action, for instance. Those didn't matter much either. The speech was too slickly phrased and deftly argued for its flaws to register for many listeners.

What stood out was a vision that we have been trapped in a blind alley for years; it has provided advantages for unscrupulous politicians, black and white; and a media trafficking in meaningless distractions. They were the words of an adult chiding unruly adolescents. The speech also contained a succinct explanation of Obama's racial worldview:

In the white community the path to a more perfect union means acknowledging that what ails the African-American community does not just exist in the minds of black people; that the legacy of discrimination—and current incidents of discrimination, while less overt than in the past—are real and must be addressed. Not just with word, but with deeds—by investing in our schools and communities; by enforcing our civil rights laws and ensuring fairness in our criminal justice system. By providing this generation with ladders of opportunity that were unavailable for previous generations. It requires all Americans to realize that your dreams do not have to come at the expense of my dreams; that investing in the health, welfare, and education of black and brown and white children will ultimately help all of America prosper.[11]

But that sentiment was camouflaged by a broader one: that blacks and whites were equally bound by the burden of race and were mutually, if not equally, damaged by it; and that the only answer was to focus on our common policy concerns. Out of this grew the mistaken notion of postracialism that flourished after the speech, despite Obama's statement that "I have never been so naive to believe that we could get beyond our racial divisions in a single election cycle or with a single candidacy, particularly a candidacy as imperfect as my own." Careful listeners heard strains of Jesse Jackson's Rainbow Coalition from two decades earlier and an even more aged belief in mutual progress that had animated the civil rights movement. In Obama's words, "We have not come from the same places but we all want to move in the same direction."

That ideals rooted in the work of the abolitionists could find flower in a presidential campaign was worthy of praise. But there was, as always, more to the story. The South Side had taught Obama that while we may all travel in the same direction, we are not necessarily moving at the same rate. Many trail behind. The theme of unity around the causes that affect us all became dominant in Obama's handling of race and complicated his relationship with black voters. Culturally speaking, Obama was blacker than an episode of *Soul Train*, speaking in the familiar tones of the black church, referencing rap music, and allowing himself amusing Ebonic lapses with African-American audiences. But politically he articulated a view that held, in essence, that what was good for America was good for black America. This may well be true, but the question was whether it was *as* good for black America. If history was any judge, it would likely not be. And on that level, the gap between America and black America had everything to do with the eventual discord between the pastor and the politician.

The issue between Wright and Obama was not two different worldviews—it was two different worlds. Obama knew something about race that neither Wright nor virtually anyone else knew in 2007: that the country was prepared to elect an African American to the highest office in the land. Wright was a product of Jim Crow; he had served in the marines at a time when the majority of black people still could not vote without fearing retribution. Obama stated that Wright's error was in holding on to a view of the country that was aged and expired. The world had changed. Obama's unique combination of experiences placed him far ahead of the idealism curve when it came to race in America. He didn't say it aloud, but the implied argument was clear: He *had* to be right because otherwise he could not be the leading contender for the Democratic presidential nomination.

The two men became a generational metaphor. The question hidden just beneath the surface of every discussion about Wright and Obama was, which of them is right? The untidy truth was that they both were. Addressing the annual National Black Writers Conference at Medgar Evers College, Cornel West offered half an accolade for the speech. "As a speech given to a racially immature society, it was brilliant. But you can't dismiss black anger as something of the past—there are a lot of young brothers and sisters out there in Brooklyn who are angry right now." It was the rare moment when fence-sitting is an act of affirmation. Comprehending the nature and velocity of change in American society during those months was difficult, particularly for African Americans struggling to reconcile the meteoric ascent of this charismatic black senator with the shrapnel of racial conflict that still cut through their own lives.

Wright made his first public comments on April 25 on *Bill Moyers Journal* and pointed out that he was a pastor and Obama a politician. He intended this facile observation to mean that he was free to speak his mind in a way that Obama was not. But it also explained why he was uniquely incapable of recognizing the magnanimity of Obama's approach to the race speech. Black preachers are afforded a phenomenal degree of power. Spending years in front of an audience that literally says amen to your opinions often leads to an attendant degree of self-import and narcissism and a low threshold for criticism. Wright had a number of virtues, but modesty was not one of them. His thirty-six-year pastorship of a massive, largely adoring congregation served to magnify Obama's mild criticism of him to nearly the level of first-degree libel.

In political terms, Obama's speech was more akin to passing Wright in a bus than throwing him under one. Joycelyn Elders, Lani Guinier, Sistah Souljah—they could've told Wright what it means to be thrown under a bus. Instead he decided to launch his ill-conceived media tour, which culminated in his self-immolation at the National Press Club on April 28.

Wright had been wildly mischaracterized and defamed by the media, and it's a natural instinct to respond to that kind of malice. You see a fire, you want to throw water on it. But Wright's situation was more akin to a grease fire, meaning it required a response that ran counter to the normal instincts. Instead, Wright opened the faucets—and the flames spread far beyond their original boundaries. The initial cycle of stories had made Wright and Trinity the target of a largely white conservative backlash. His appearance at the National Press Club generated a second chorus of condemnation. But the jeers were now coming from both whites and blacks. He had started out with the enmity of misinformed whites who knew him only through the manipulated soundbites that had been looped ad nauseam but were then dying down. He then garnered the contempt of blacks who accused him of attempting to derail the Obama campaign. Others felt, quite simply, that the imperative to speak truth to power would become an obstacle to Obama's actually attaining power. Author Bakari Kitwana assessed it as part of a generational conflict, for reasons somewhat different than those elucidated by Obama:

> Jeremiah Wright's apparent undermining of Barack Obama's campaign gets to the heart of an ongoing battle that has been heating up in the Black community since Obama first announced his candidacy. By entertaining the mainstream media that has been quick to pull down Obama, Wright is displaying a dangerous disregard for Obama's historic candidacy. But he's not doing it on purpose. Jeremiah Wright, like others of his generation, is only treating Barack Obama's candidacy like the youthful pipe dream that he always thought it was.[12]

Writing in the *New York Times*, Bob Herbert accused Wright of vengefully sabotaging Obama at the Press Club; Errol Louis of the New York *Daily News* gave Wright the benefit of the doubt and said that "he couldn't have done more damage to Obama if he tried."[13] E-mails circulated referring to the event as "black-on-black crime" and speculating that Wright was secretly on Hillary Clinton's payroll.

It must have been unspeakably difficult for Wright to see his work and reputation be defamed for weeks on end, but he entered the press conference with a flawed agenda: The commercial media do not specialize in reconciliation. Wright dismissed Obama's words as political rhetoric and defended his "Goddamn America" statements. But the content was nearly irrelevant; what mattered was the way those words would be consumed, filtered, repackaged, and distributed. He was like a man who has lost a hundred dollars to a card hustler and believes he can break even by playing again.

Wright was buoyed by a false confidence in his own communication skills. He was a brilliant preacher, but a podium is not a pulpit. He moved directly from an amen corner into an arena where people are paid to be skeptical. His press conference had the boomerang effect of turning Obama's Philadelphia speech into a liability. He painted Obama into a corner, after Obama had tried to place Wright in context.

Ironically, less than twenty-four hours later Wright got to see what a real rejection looked like, as Barack and Michelle Obama formally resigned from the church and the candidate dismissed him as "not the man he knew." In closing the door on Trinity, Obama was necessarily closing the door on a portion of his own history, though he remained widely beloved in the church. But in another sense it signified that he was no longer bound to the institution on the South Side—and a step closer to the institution at 1600 Pennsylvania Avenue.

CHAPTER 3

The Jesse Problem

THE BLACK PRESIDENT AND THE
PRESIDENT OF BLACK AMERICA

IN JANUARY 2008 I wrote an op-ed for the *Washington Post* pointing out that the most fascinating element of current events was not that a black man had a credible shot at winning the White House, but that he would do so over the active opposition of the civil rights establishment: most notably, the awkward, arm's-length embrace that Jesse Jackson had offered Obama and the passive-aggressive public commentary he'd made about the senator.

The piece generated more than six hundred replies, about 95 percent of which were critical of Jackson and other civil rights leaders for their treatment of Obama. One observed:

> Thank you for putting in writing the thought that I have not been able to properly articulate [regarding] Obama's bid for the presidency. In my opinion the media-appointed, so-called "Black Leadership" is so busy holding on to their torch/throne that they keep us from progressing to the next level.

Another added:

I have felt for years that [Jackson and Sharpton] for the
most part, are pseudo leaders of the Black community
in America. They only appear when and where they
aren't necessarily needed . . . when was the last time
any of these men actually made a real difference?[14]

Jackson replied in short order with a commentary in the *Post*
under the title "Obama Is Not a Threat." The piece was more or
less a history lesson about how the civil rights movement had
opened the door for Barack Obama, but it largely sidestepped
the implications that his election would invalidate, or severely
impede, the old business model—the one in which black politicians and civil rights leaders acted as brokers delivering African-
American support to the white political establishment. On election
night in Chicago, an iconic photograph was taken of Jesse Jackson
standing in Grant Park, his face stained by the tears that openly
flowed down his cheeks. It should have been a moment of clear
emotional resonance—a man had stood with Martin Luther
King Jr. witnessing the most audacious fulfillment of his dream.
Instead the picture evoked a more sardonic mental headline: *Why
is this man crying?*

Jackson embodied the struggles and sacrifices to open doors
but also the ambivalence and envy that arise when someone
new and talented actually walks through them. These two poles
perhaps more than anything else explain Jackson's tortured relationship with Barack Obama.

Jackson, like many a gifted egotist in history, finds no distinction between his own interests and those of the people whom he
purportedly leads. (At one point in his career he routinely referred to himself as "the president of black America.") If you
stand up long enough and offer your own biography as testament in enough arenas, the lines begin to go hazy. That explains
why Jackson's personal animosity toward Obama would, almost invariably, be framed in terms of a threat to black America's best interests. Still, the speed with which those dynamics

diminished Jackson's standing—and legacy—was jarring. At the start of the campaign season, Jackson was an underheralded pioneer who had laid the groundwork for Obama's success. From there he descended to the first black leader known to publicly threaten the well-being of a presidential candidate's genitals.

In its slick vocabulary, hip-hop reviles a creature known as a hater. In this context, *hate* (not to be confused with *hatred*) is the highest form of jealousy. The hater is incapable of recognizing or appreciating the accomplishments of others, because in the zero-sum game of success, one man's glory is another man's setback. In the days after the castration story broke, the number of times the term *hater* was invoked to explain Jackson was probably correlated with his waning significance to younger African Americans. The day after his desire to "cut his nuts off" comment became public knowledge, a seventeen-year-old Harlemite used the term to explain the reverend's actions. "He is just a hater who just wants to get his name in the paper," she explained to me.

In fairness to Jackson, hate probably does not explain the entire palette of motivations at play. The political ascent of Barack Obama stood at odds with all that we—black and white, poor and wealthy, conservative and liberal—thought we knew about this country. None of us knew what to make of it. The week after the Iowa caucuses, the *Final Call*—organ of the Nation of Islam and consistent chronicler of white wrongdoing—offered this incongruent image: a photo of Louis Farrakhan and the caption IS AMERICA CHANGING HER ATTITUDE?[15]

We were surrounded by less-than-inspirational realities: an African American with no criminal record fared about as well in the job market as a white person who had been convicted of a crime. The death of Sean Bell at the hands of New York Police officers and the tragedy of Hurricane Katrina remained fresh in our minds. Jackson's bewilderment simply took far less graceful forms than that of most of his peers. He, more than any other living leader, was responsible for birthing the opportunities Obama seized, but during the summer he seemed unable to decide whether he wanted to be cast as Madonna or Medea.

Here was a definition of ambivalence. If you Googled the names of the two most significant black presidential candidates in American history, the search would yield successive hits that read "Jesse Jackson Backs Barack Obama" and "Jesse Jackson on Barack Obama: I wanna cut his nuts off." Jackson's public performance recalled the late career of Joe Louis—he was knocked through ropes not so much by Rocky Marciano's right hand as by his own hubris. Joe Louis was a hero to the young Jackson (as he was to much of Jackson's generation), but that end-stage Louis, unintentionally caricaturing the Brown Bomber, came awkwardly close to repeating itself with Jackson. There are plenty of explanations, though no excuses, for the reverend's public demise but they can be distilled down to this: The only thing less appealing than having one's obituary written is still being around to read it.

Jackson has never shrunk from metaphorical renderings of his life, but he probably does not appreciate the one now affixed to him: symbol of the declining status of his generation of black leadership. Indicators suggested that some personal low-pressure system was brewing inside Jackson long before the tempest made landfall in July 2008. Initially cool toward the junior senator from his home state, Jackson endorsed Obama in March 2007, at a point when few expected the campaign to succeed.

The tensions surfaced early. In September 2007 Jackson remarked that the senator was "acting like he's white." The issue was the case of the Jena Six, a group of black Louisiana youth charged with attempted murder following a racially motivated school fight. As nooses were being hung on nearby trees, the specter of lynch law was re-awakened. The case was tailor-made for the bullhorn brigade in which Jackson and Sharpton served as field officers. Obama's office offered legal support, but Jackson charged that the candidate's response had been lacking. His comment was reported in the state newspaper in South Carolina and on Fox News, neither of which was a large or reputable enough venue to make a dent with blacks. Still it was a sideways reintroduction of the tiresome "black enough" dialogue that had dogged Obama the previous spring.[16]

In late November Jackson used his column in the *Chicago Sun-Times* to assert that most of the Democratic presidential candidates were ignoring African American concerns. "The Democratic candidates—with the exception of John Edwards, who opened his campaign in New Orleans' Ninth Ward and has made addressing poverty central to his campaign—have virtually ignored the plight of African Americans in this country." Obama was damned by implication in Jackson's charge that "when thousands of African Americans marched in protest in Jena, La., not one candidate showed up." As a two-time presidential candidate himself, Jackson knew that Jena represented a racial minefield, one in which the risk of misinterpretation and the possible liabilities were high.[17]

The contours of the generational conflict emerged a week later when Congressman Jesse Jackson Jr. defended Obama from his father's charges in the pages of the *Sun-Times*:

> As a national co-chairman of Sen. Barack Obama's presidential campaign, I've been a witness to Obama's powerful, consistent and effective advocacy for African Americans. He is deeply rooted in the black community, having fought for social justice and economic inclusion throughout his life. On the campaign trail—as he's done in the U.S. Senate and the state Legislature before that—Obama has addressed many of the issues facing African Americans out of personal conviction, rather than political calculation.[18]

Later, in that middle period after he had publicly criticized his father but had no clue that he would soon have to do so again in even harsher terms, the congressman explained his position to me. "I was very critical of my father and others who have demanded that Barack Obama pass a certain kind of litmus test in our community before the Iowa caucuses. There aren't enough

Black folks in Iowa to give a pro-Black speech. Their position was 'prove to us that you're down with the soul brothers'—in the middle of Nevada, where there's mostly Latinos. That's not how politics is done."[19]

Five weeks after Jackson Sr.'s commentary, Barack Obama won the Iowa caucuses. It was hailed as an unprecedented moment in American politics. The prevailing idea was that by winning in a state that is 94 percent white, where no African American had ever been elected to statewide office, Obama had crossed a threshold. The victory translated into immediate credibility with black voters in South Carolina and provided the punditocracy with a buffet of talking points. But beneath the confetti was another issue. The victory marked a tremendous step forward but was also consistent with the little-recognized truth that African Americans often stand a better chance with white voters in states where there are few blacks. In Mississippi, where African Americans represent 36 percent of the population, most white voters would not come within a cotton field of a black candidate.

Iowa also highlighted the extent to which Obama's ascent had begun to overshadow Jackson's accomplishments. January 3, 2008, was not the first time an African-American candidate had won in an overwhelmingly white state. In 1988 Jesse Jackson had won in Vermont, a state that is less than 1 percent black—a fact that eluded virtually all the commentary that appeared post-Iowa. In the halo moment of Iowa, the details of history slipped beneath the surface—a bitter moment of amnesia of which Jackson was certainly aware.

As the Iowa returns rolled in, Jackson was backstage at CNN's New York studio with two younger men. Baratunde Thurston and Michael Washington represented the generation whose lives were shaped by the political and social struggles Jackson had been waging before they were born. On January 5, 2008 Thurston, a Harvard-educated blogger, and Washington, an organizer with Harlem for Obama, were scheduled to appear with Jackson on *Out in the Open* with host Rick Sanchez.

Backstage Jackson made comments that previewed the arguments he would repeatedly deploy against his unsanctioned heir. Obama was selling people on hope, Jackson pointed out, but "hope is one thing and substance is another." When the show aired, both Thurston and Washington spoke movingly about what Obama's victory meant to them as black men and to American society at large. Hours afterward Thurston recorded a video blog in which he admitted to crying when he heard Obama's Iowa speech. "I felt, for a rare moment in my life, like an actual American," he pointed out. Weeks later when Michelle Obama expressed that sentiment, it would be hung around her neck, but the feeling was widely held in the precincts of black America. For many, especially those who had not lived through the tumult of the civil rights era, that moment, in which a black man gave a victory speech in the season's first primary, was an induction of sorts.

Jackson's comments to Sanchez, though, carried a different tone. "Faith," he said, "is the substance of things hoped for." The preacher engaged in the biblical game of the dozens. He ticked off a list of problems in black America: "infant mortality, health care gap, income gap, access to capital gap, subprime exploitation. So hope and substance must come together. We must connect hope with substance." In the context of charges that Obama was vague on policy specifics, this was a serious critique. Jackson had also violated an unspoken rule of politics— that you do not publicly criticize a candidate you have endorsed. The damning implication of his words was that the hope Obama offered was insubstantial, though had Obama offered *hopeless substance*—an array of agenda specifics—it might have satisfied the preacher but would have doomed his broader candidacy.

Obama's actual vagueness wasn't due to lack of content but rather was part of the genius of his campaign. He was not all things to all people, but he managed to be more things to most. He shrewdly used the blank-screen effect to his advantage. In a campaign cycle in which people thirsted for a new direction,

Obama '08 became the shorthand reference for it. So deliciously ambiguous was his theme of change that it invited each person to invest their own meanings in it—and by extension, in him.

The change doctrine proved so permeable, so viral, that even the most faithless practitioner of the democratic creed, the most lapsed citizen, knew to associate it with Obama. *Change* meant whatever you thought it meant: from Republican to Democrat, from partisan to ecumenical, from a president who slouches to one with the posture of a pharaoh. And for a great many, it meant change from the old-model retail black leaders to something different. Jesse Jackson understood this better than most.

But whatever the implications of Obama's hope politic, on *Out in the Open* Michael Washington called Jesse on his faint praise, asking repeatedly if the reverend intended to support Obama. The segment ended with Jackson defensively citing his endorsement of Obama, and the three men took pictures together in the studio. But across the generational divide, Jackson's words made him appear a hater of the first magnitude.

Later that night in his video blog Thurston respectfully dissented with Jackson. "I've had my differences with Jesse Jackson, but I can't deny that I'm able to express those differences because of what he and his contemporaries have done and ancestors before him did. I was honored to meet him. Backstage he said hope was one thing and substance was another, and he repeated that on the show . . . I was a little deferential, and at the same time he was wrong. Obama is not just hope, not just talk. Iowa proved that."

When I spoke to Jackson in June, shortly after Obama clinched the nomination, the reverend was Beltway cool, offering a verbal press release of praiseful quotations. Asked about the generational divide and the 1988 campaign, he smoothly sidestepped any discussion of tensions between himself and Obama. But privately he unsuccessfully pitched magazine editors, suggesting that they assign stories on the way his 1988 campaign had opened the door for Obama.

The ensuing weeks depleted Jackson's finesse reserves. To the trained eye, it was apparent two weeks prior to the castration comment that some private breaker in Jackson's circuitry was about to flip. When Jesse took the stage at the Rainbow-PUSH conference recognizing the twentieth anniversary of his last presidential run, he surrounded himself with the pageantry that the digital narrators of the media had denied him. David Murray, a *Vibe* magazine reporter who covered the gathering, noted a distant thunder rumble, even if the storm clouds had not yet fully formed:

> Two strong ideas jutted out: first it was taken as a happy fact that Obama is going to be the next president of the United States. And—just as importantly, it seemed on that Saturday morning—this marvelous moment in American politics is not a dream bubble in some post-racial Obamalogue; it's merely the latest of many fixed footprints on a not-yet-nearly-finished civil rights slog in which Rev. Jackson figures prominently.[20]

In his speech Jackson offered Obama a hater-ish caution not to ascribe Obama's ascension to the foresight of the Democratic Party and waxed theological about the importance of giving credit where it was due. That bit of résumé flashing would have been beneath Jackson had he not already lowered himself so far.

In one sense, Jesse Jackson's July 2008 threat to Obama's reproductive organs was part of a lineage of American slip-ups, akin to John McCain confusing Sunni and Shia, or Obama forgetting to place his hand over his heart during the national anthem. Speak long enough in public, and you will invariably make a fool of yourself. But for reasons that preceded Obama's presidential campaign, Jackson's gaffe could not be dismissed as simply another politician speaking out of turn. In the same conversation in which he made his inflammatory castration comment, Jackson also referred to Obama as a "nigga." And no matter how colloquially he intended it, Jackson had ensnared himself in a trap. The preceding year he had assailed the rap artist Nas for attempting to title his upcoming album *Nigger*. Jackson, who had almost single-handedly driven the shift to the term *African American* in the 1980s, was quoted as saying, "The title using the 'N' word is morally offensive and socially distasteful. Nas has the right to degrade and denigrate in the name of free speech, but there is no honor in it." In the midst of the epithet wars, the Mississippi-based rap artist David Banner recorded a scathing uppercut of a song titled "So Special" in which he referred to Jackson, who had fathered a child outside his marriage, as a "deadbeat dad." Nor could it be forgotten that the NAACP had publicly buried the word a year earlier. By using the word to refer to Obama, Jackson didn't reincarnate it so much as offer a toast to its good health.

The response to his "nigga" comment about Obama was swift and furious. In interviews Nas declared, "We don't need Jesse, we got Barack." Rapper Ludacris recorded a song in which he challenged Jackson's sincerity for "talking slick and apologizing," telling the older man, "If you said it, you meant it."[21]

If Jackson had placed himself in the crosshairs of history by mumbling that radioactive six-letter word (or a five-letter colloquial variation), his comment about castration all but pulled the trigger. In the days after they became public, Jackson's words played out in the broader society as a moment of locker-room jive, but African Americans consistently wondered how he could have been so historically obtuse. In a community already on high alert, fearing for Obama's safety, Jackson's comment brought immediate flashbacks to the era of lynching, in which black men were routinely castrated in public. His words deftly conjured that recurrent nightmare; but had any white observer been clueless enough to utter them, Jackson himself would almost certainly have protested and demanded an apology.

Jackson did offer an apology. Of sorts. The reverend's handlers might have done well to remind him that a sincere apology does not contain the word *if*. For his part, Jackson offered a conditional sorry, one hinged upon the possibility that his words had caused harm. But less than twenty-four hours later he appeared on CNN and rearticulated his "hope and substance" shtick, arguing that Obama's faith-based initiatives couldn't work if the churches were located in poor neighborhoods or the congregation suffered from unemployment. Jesse Jr. reprised his role as Obama's prime supporter in the Jackson household and issued a sharply worded condemnation of his father's words:

> I'm deeply outraged and disappointed in Reverend Jackson's reckless statements about Senator Barack Obama. His divisive and demeaning comments about the presumptive Democratic nominee—and I believe the next president of the United States—contradict his inspiring and courageous career.[22]

The hedged apology did little to stem the tide of condemnation against Jackson. The more generous observers pointed to the fact that Jackson had uttered his words off the air and questioned the ethics of publicizing remarks that were not made on the record. But Jackson had been speaking on Fox News—a network whose coverage of racial issues was dubious at best. The most benign assessment that Jackson could hope for was that he'd been trapped in an electronic noose—and had been given enough rope to hang himself.

AMONG HISTORIANS there is a professional sin known as presentism. The presentist looks at an old man's stooped shoulders in 2008 and imagines that his appearance was the same in 1968. He imports the values of the contemporary world wholesale into the past and scales the dimensions of history's actors downward.

If Jesse Louis Jackson's shoulders appear to be stooped, it is mainly because few of us recognize the workings of history but also because the contrast between the dynamic advocate of black advancement and the aged and bitter hater is so great. The tragedy lies not in people forgetting the specifics of one's greatness but that one had even been capable of it.

By 2007 Jackson had already become so disreputable that commentators openly wondered whether his ambivalence toward Obama was actually to the campaign's benefit. During one heated stretch of the primaries, *Saturday Night Live* ran a cartoon in which Obama dispatches Jackson (along with Al Sharpton) on increasingly ridiculous junkets to nonexistent countries in order to prevent them from campaigning for him at home.

By that point the younger Jackson's aura was almost completely absent from his bearing. The Jackson of 1984 had had charisma and intelligence that made him one of *Time* magazine's most admired Americans. But the larger-than-life icon had been run through the rinse cycle of history and had come out slightly smaller than the times.

I crossed paths with Jackson as a college freshman in 1988 and witnessed his force of personality firsthand. His presidential run was just beginning to gather the electoral momentum that would alarm the democratic establishment and Michael Dukakis, the eventual nominee. He appeared on a panel of candidates. Watching Jackson address the caucus was roughly akin to watching Dave Winfield take batting practice. During the Q&A someone asked the candidates about their plans to support black colleges. The others mumbled prosaic answers about education as "the great equalizer" and "opening the doors to opportunity." With Rosa Parks seated at the front of the room as a living reminder of civil rights history, Jackson answered that his first means of supporting black colleges would be to continue sending his children to them. He then ticked off the list of institutions his children attended and finally cited his own alma mater, North Carolina A&T University. If his response lacked policy details, he had made his point to a crowd whose own educational pedigrees included places like Morgan State, Grambling, Morehouse, and Lincoln University. The obvious subtext to his statements: I am one of your own. The room erupted into chants of "Run, Jesse, run!"

That Jackson, the one who so easily mastered an audience and inspired the belief that he represented the best of their aspirations, was part of a grand American tradition. Ambition is the closest thing to a national faith in America, a creed that is the opposite of Zen, holding that if you can grasp all you've reached for, then you aren't reaching far enough. Jackson and Obama are members of the same fraternity of ambition; when Jackson addressed the 1988 Democratic National Convention, he was the same age that Obama was when he formally accepted the party's nomination in 2008. For reasons that are both grand and intricate, both men were seen as arrogant upstarts whose unruly aspirations would cause headaches for preordained Democratic nominees.

On the strength of his presidential campaigns, Jesse Jackson, more than any other figure in national politics, was responsible for transforming African Americans from the Democratic Party's largest voting bloc into one of its most powerful interest groups.

In his first campaign Jackson claimed victory in two primaries and came in second in five. But his mere presence in the race had something of a high-tide effect. In the former Confederate states, black registration increased by 30 percent—a surge that lifted the electoral fortunes of Democrats, black and white, running down-ticket during the general election. Four years later Jackson won thirteen primaries, amassed some seven million votes, and walked into the Democratic National Convention in Atlanta with one third of the delegates. Jackson's campaign was also a kind of triple-A team for upcoming black political talent. Ron Brown, Donna Brazile, and Alexis Herman, all of whom went on to figure prominently in the party's upper reaches, were connected to Jackson's presidential efforts, as were many of the blacks whom Bill Clinton would later tap for positions within his administration.

Jackson and Obama share ties that are historical, personal,

and political. For one, their families are bound by the networks among Chicago's black strivers. Michelle Obama and Jesse's older daughter Santita were childhood friends on Chicago's South Side. (Santita Jackson sang at the Obamas' wedding and is godmother to their older daughter, Malia.) Jesse Jackson Jr. was one of Obama's earliest supporters and a national co-chair of his campaign. But in 2000, when Obama attempted to unseat Congressman Bobby Rush, Jackson endorsed the incumbent, who handed Obama a crushing defeat in the primary.

More substantively, Jackson's two presidential campaigns were directly responsible for the party reforms that made Obama's nomination possible. In exchange for his support of Dukakis, Jackson demanded that the party adopt a proportional system of allocating delegates. Under the old system, a candidate who received the majority of votes in a state won all the delegates. The proportional system enhanced the prospects of minority representation among the state delegations. Jackson's team also argued for changing the minimum threshold for qualifying in a race. Ron Walters, the Howard University political science professor who helped plan strategy for Jackson's races, explained it as part of an overall push to democratize the party and enhance the power of black voters:

> We were not for the high threshold in order to achieve delegates in the congressional districts. At the time they had a 20 percent threshold. Because of our protest they brought it down 15 percent . . . What I found, just in doing an analysis, is that because blacks were stacked up in the inner city, we were trading out a lot of what I call excess voters. So, Jackson had an impact on this whole business of the delegates.

Jackson Jr. echoed that theme:

> In 2008 Barack Obama did not have to run for president demanding that the party be fair. But if Barack

ran in 2008 without Reverend Jackson having run, we
would still have had a winner-take-all system. He'd
be demanding the Democrats give him his fair share of
delegates.[23]

In addition to frustrating the attempts of pundits to keep
track of the delegate count, the proportional voting system
that was adopted following Jackson's 1984 campaign had an
additional effect: It blunted the effect of the large, delegate-
rich states on the overall race. Twenty years after Jackson's
campaign, Obama was able to string together enough victories in small states to effectively equal the number of delegates
that states like California and New York delivered to Hillary
Clinton.

Examine Jackson's campaigns, and you begin to see the DNA
of an Obama candidacy. The overlaps and echoes in the two
campaigns exceed coincidence. Both Jackson and Obama tied
their political fortunes to the buoyant theme of "hope." Jackson's rallying cry, "Keep hope alive," stood as a counterpoint to
the eight years of Reaganism that had gutted morale among
African Americans and progressives. Obama's version of hope
was wielded against the backdrop of the Bush administration's
secret detentions, calculated political retaliation, and overcast
realism.

Moreover Jackson's hope-politic was deeply rooted in his
own experience as a member of the clergy. On another level,
hope referenced the gritty optimism of the black church tradition that had birthed the civil rights movement, one that is unconcerned with whether the glass is half empty or half full
but recognizes that simply having a glass is a starting place.
Obama's ancestors had not been slaves, and ironically, his critics saw part of his appeal to whites in that fact: He did not
evoke the sense of guilt that other black Americans did. But
whatever the particulars of his lineage, Obama was clearly impacted by the slave-derived religious tradition thriving inside
Trinity's sanctuary.

Jesse Jackson grew up inside that tradition, declaring in his early adolescence that he would become a preacher. As an aide to Dr. King, he saw the ways in which it could yield immense moral and social power. While King sought to harness that power in the service of social reform, Jackson's 1984 campaign attempted to use it as a direct political force. The Rainbow Coalition he set out to build was really a brand of social gospel—mercy upon the poor and the afflicted—mixed with old-fashioned American populism.

More often than not, populist politics had appealed to the lowest racial denominator: Jackson's unique contribution in the two campaigns was to re-envision populism as a means of cross-racial alliance building. At the same time his candidacy, particularly in 1984, was largely symbolic. As such, he could afford to appeal to the progressive edges of the Democratic Party. Obama, for his part, faced a higher bar simply because he ran as a sitting senator who fully intended to win his party's nomination.

Days after Obama won the Democratic Party nomination, Jackson recalled a story about his first campaign trip to Iowa. He encountered a farmer who was beset with debt and struggling to hold on to his farm. Jackson told him that poor policy making, not poor blacks, was the source of his woes. He laid out the case for the common folk of all colors—the "locked-outs," as the campaign called them—working together. But the farmer reportedly told Jackson that he just couldn't bring himself to vote for a black man. "He was not able to," Jackson said, "but twenty years later, his sons and daughters were." More specifically, his college-educated, environmentally conscious, anti–Iraq War children were able to envision a black man as chief executive.

There were other ties as well. Political scientist Ron Walters, who had served as one of Jackson's strategists, pointed out:

> The way in which Jackson conducted his campaign was also unique because . . . it conducted, at the same time, a vigorous voter registration drive. That is precisely what Barack Obama is doing right now. And we did it

because of the philosophy of expanding the base of the
party; [we knew] there were lots of people who were
potentially Democrats who were not registered and
therefore did not vote, and we thought that was part of
the key to our being successful.[24]

Even before he clinched the nomination, Obama was vowing to
compete in all fifty states during the general election. That was,
in some ways, an echo of Democratic National Committee chair
Howard Dean's desire to broaden the electoral map, but it was also
based on the realization that his candidacy could have extraor-
dinary appeal to African Americans and increase their registration and turnout enough to make a serious difference in states that
traditionally voted Republican.

In 1984 Jackson's success and burgeoning impact upon Democratic politics placed other black leadership in a delicate position. Stalwarts who had come up in the movement with him were
forced to choose between a campaign that seemed to be the next
installment in the The Movement and a chance to exercise influence among the white power brokers within the party. The
predicament was itself an echo of history. In 1967 Dr. King's
decision to criticize the Vietnam War nearly factionalized his
circle of advisers. On the heels of Lyndon B. Johnson's nation-
changing support for the Civil Rights and Voting Rights acts, it
would have been politic for King to remain silent on the war.
Had he been interested in raising his line of credit with the president, King would have tacitly or publicly supported the war.
The difficulty lay in deciding the lengths to which one would go,
the moral compromises one would countenance, to gain political advantage.

The moral lines of Jackson's 1984 candidacy were not nearly
so stark: Walter Mondale, who was almost certain to win the
nomination, was a pro-civil-rights liberal. But Jackson was un-
questionably the voice of the least and the last, the people whom
the movement initially set out to empower. Coretta Scott King's
endorsement of Mondale created a small backlash. Though she

had been a steward and protector of her husband's legacy, a group of black Jackson supporters at the 1984 San Francisco convention shouted her down. Andrew Young, whose elevation to UN ambassador during the Carter administration made him the most highly placed of King's former lieutenants, was cool toward Jackson's initial run. And when he did offer an endorsement, it came via a private note, not a public podium. In that way 1984 was a dress rehearsal for the left-footed choreography of endorsements and reversals that marked the 2008 primary season.

Obama fared better. The Congressional Black Caucus was split almost evenly between endorsements for him and for Hillary Clinton; as he closed in on the nomination, a series of late-inning defections took place. Like Jackson in 1988, Obama carried the districts of many representatives who had endorsed his opponent, leaving them vulnerable to challengers.

There were other symmetries between the two men's campaigns. Jackson's 1984 convention speech, nearly as iridescent as the coalition he hoped to build, was shot through with biblical themes of fallibility and forgiveness. When Jackson implored his critics to charge his low moments "to my head and not to my heart," he was alluding both to his infamous reference to New York as "Hymietown" and to his previous association with Louis Farrakhan.[25]

In the tempest that followed the January 1984 publication of the *Washington Post* article in which the "Hymietown" epithet appeared, Farrakhan gave a speech declaring journalist Milton Coleman a traitor and threatening his life. The fevered rhetoric inflamed the controversy. Jackson faced a double bind: Farrakhan was trying to intimidate the media that Jackson was attempting to court for damage control. At that point, Jackson and Farrakhan were seen as the two most prominent heirs of Dr. King and Malcolm X respectively. Farrakhan's Nation of Islam had provided Jackson with security when he was denied Secret Service protection, and the group's rank and file were people Jackson was hoping to bring into the political process. Outside the Nation membership, Farrakhan held symbolic value to the communities in Chicago that Jackson counted as his base.

Calls for Jackson to denounce Farrakhan began to make the media circuit. Jackson demurred and attempted to place Farrakhan's words in context. The result was a punctuated crisis in which pieces of the Farrakhan story emerged at regular intervals and reignited the embers of a fading story. After weeks of trying to referee the situation, Jackson finally denounced Farrakhan's comments—a step that was, at the time, seen as yet another black leader being compromised by the inexorable will of the white media establishment.

That same cycle was replayed when Jeremiah Wright's 9/11 response came to light. Detached from its context, the snippet presented a concave image of Wright. Wright's words stuttering across the news spectrum constituted the first major crisis of Obama's candidacy. Obama went several steps farther than Jackson, however. Where Jackson sought to simply contextualize Farrakhan, Obama offered his brilliant Philadelphia race speech, which placed the country, its citizens, its leadership, and the media reporting the story into context.

The Wright and Farrakhan stories shared a curiously similar media arc: Both involved a black presidential campaign that was nearly derailed by the feverish rhetoric of a Chicago-based black nationalist religious leader. Initially both men refused to distance themselves from the comments that sparked the firestorm, only to see the story gain intensity. And both eventually severed ties with the subject of the controversy.

Obama was more fortunate (if that is the term) than most: Black voters directed their ire overwhelmingly at the pastor, amid speculation that Wright was some kind of Trojan horse in a clergy collar. But this was largely because Obama was a household name, while Wright, despite his decades-long record of community work, was not particularly well known outside black religious circles. But blogger Mark Anthony Neal was moved to remark:

At the very least, Senator Obama owed it to his constituency to be more publicly honest about why Trinity
United mattered to him and his family . . . Obama decided to sever ties with Trinity United and, to some extent, the myriad black communities that will continue to
find value in the faith and practice of churches like
Trinity United. Those same communities might be left
to wonder what other aspects of their existence Senator
Obama might be willing to "sell off" in the name of
political survival.[26]

On another level, both Obama and Jackson owed at least part
of their political fortunes to those lightning rods. The Trinity
membership provided Obama with an important base for his
early political efforts. Farrakhan played a crucial role in Jackson's emergence as a national figure. In 1983 Navy Lieutenant
Robert Goodman was shot down over Syria and spent thirty
days in a Syrian prison. In a moment of brilliant insubordina-
tion, Jackson put together a team of grassroots diplomats, flew
to Syria, and negotiated Goodman's release. Louis Farrakhan
traveled to Syria as part of that delegation and made a lingering
impression on the Syrians when he led them in traditional Muslim prayer in flawless Arabic.

Jackson also knew that with the Syrians he could shrewdly
leverage both his own charisma and his own racial identity. His
dark skin was a passport of sorts, an unspoken reminder of the
subordinate position that blacks occupied in the United States
and a common ground with others who felt exploited by U.S.
dominion.

Nor are the men's similar experiences confined to politics.
The most influential dynamic in the early lives of both Jackson
and Obama was paternal abandonment. That experience surfaced in both men's rhetoric as a kind of personal claim to public life (though Jackson's personal excesses made that claim, at
the very least, extremely complicated). On the campaign trail

Obama made frequent reference to being "raised in a single-parent home," though his mother had remarried and his grandparents often stepped into the void left by his absent father. In South Carolina, Obama relayed the inspirational story of a talented young student who had overcome a series of obstacles to achieve academic success and who, "like me, never really knew his father."

Most significantly, Obama's memoir—written before he entered politics—chronicles his search for his father and, by extension, his identity as an African American man. Jackson, in his incandescent 1988 convention address, reminded listeners that they saw "the house he was running for, but not the house I'm running from." That house was next door to the one where his father lived with his wife. Jackson was born to an unwed teenage mother who had herself been born to an unwed teenage mother. The circumstances of his birth were cause for scandal: Noah Robinson, a man in his mid-thirties, had seduced his sixteen-year-old neighbor after his own marriage failed to produce any children. Marshall Frady, Jackson's biographer, has argued that, having grown up fatherless, Jackson eventually came to see his relationship to the broader black community in paternal terms. At the zenith of Jackson's public life he seized upon that experience, inverted it, and wielded it as his deepest qualification:

> I understand. I know abandonment, and people being mean to you, and saying you're nothing and nobody and can never be anything. Jesse Jackson is my third name. I'm adopted. When I had no name, my grandmother gave me her name. My name was Jesse Burns till I was twelve. So I wouldn't have blank space, she gave me a name to hold me over. I understand when nobody knows your name. I wasn't born in a hospital. Mama didn't have insurance. I was born in a three-room house, bathroom in the backyard, slop jar by the bed, no hot and cold running water. I understand . . . Every one of these funny labels they put on you, those

of you who are watching this broadcast tonight in the projects, on the corners, I understand. Call you outcast, low down, you can't make it, you're nothing, you're no-body, subclass, underclass; when you see my name [go] in nomination, your name goes in nomination.[27]

The fatherless household is a statistical minefield for black boys in particular. Yet both Jackson and Obama drew on that experience as a tailwind to navigate in the world. Thus witnessing the two men clash over the content of a Father's Day speech is a metaphor so heavy-handed that it can exist only in the world of politics.

In any community with a history of exploitation, privacy takes on exaggerated dimensions. Yet "airing dirty laundry," providing ammunition to those hostile outside forces, is the most serious of racial felonies. The contention swirling around the address that Barack Obama gave on Father's Day 2008 had little to do with its actual content—and few within the church appeared to dissent at the time. Black critics later complained that he should have used that occasion to praise those fathers who are devoted to their families, but the real issue was that Obama appeared to be chastising black people as a means of scoring points with whites.

Eric Easter, who had been press secretary during Jackson's 1988 campaign, summed up that perspective when he wrote that Obama's Father's Day speech

> focused most aggressively on the pathologies of a disturbing percentage of black men . . . As with Jackson's example, it's not what you say, it's all about where, when, and to whom . . . The fear among critics is that the real audience that day was not the Black people in the pews at all, but the white people in the middle. Whether that was Obama's intention is impossible to know, but the event smacked of calculated political expediency that troubled more than a few.

Even that observation did not get at the entirety of the situation. A black man running for president, one critic wrote,

> has ventured into areas of criticism only he could get
> away with, unabashedly calling problems of individual
> conduct that bedevil the black community and the
> quality of urban life by extension. No white politician
> could presently challenge black people to get off drugs
> and raise the babies they make, to stop being lack-
> adaisical in public school, to work their way out of
> problems rather than merely whine as they sullenly ac-
> cept their conditions. Any white politician so bold would
> be shouted down as racist, or as one given to dangerous
> generalizations.[28]

That comment comes not from a white observer of Obama's
2008 Father's Day speech but from a black writer, Stanley Crouch,
in response to a speech Jackson gave in 1988. While simultaneously demanding deeper inclusion in American society, Jackson
had frequently chastised African Americans with statements
like "the rising use of drugs and babies making babies and violence is cutting away our opportunity."

Jackson's calls for moral uplift, parental responsibility, hard
work, and education have been consistent in his three decades
of public commentary. In 1993 he remarked, "There is nothing
more painful to me at this stage in my life than to walk down the
street and hear footsteps and start thinking about robbery—
then look around and see somebody white and feel relieved."
Given the charged subject of black crime, those words are arguably far more inflammatory than the speech Obama gave fifteen years later. All this made Jackson's rhetorical assault on
Obama seem motivated by more base concerns than Obama's
alleged condescension.

Jackson's reaction was also complicated by his precarious
personal life. Karin Stanford, Jackson's former mistress and the

mother of his nine-year-old daughter, took to the pages of the *National Enquirer* to declare that for the reverend, Obama's call for paternal responsibility struck too close to home. Radio host and critic Larry Elder appeared on CNN the day after the castration story broke and said, "Perhaps Jackson is offended because he is one of the fathers Obama was talking about—he does have a child out of wedlock."

Prior to that point Jackson had, with some merit, argued that his own campaign marked not only a chronological midpoint between King's assassination and Obama's nomination, but a spiritual and social one as well. That the two men's addresses to the Democratic National Convention would be compared was inevitable. Jackson's words from 1988 contain a kind of raw hymnal beauty, a blues ethic that Obama's 2004 speech lacked. If Jackson presented America an invoice, Obama delivered a thank-you note, a commentary from the immigrant's son ("In a tolerant America, your name is no barrier to success"). For this reason one was hailed as postracial and the other disdained as megaracial. Obama was speaking as an American; Jackson, as a man who had spent forty-three years trying to become one.

Jackson's 1988 speech began with a pedigree of the civil rights movement; he acknowledged Rosa Parks in the audience and pointed out that King's body lay just a few miles away from the Atlanta convention center. His presence was insistent, there to collect on an overdue note from America at large. By that point, however, liberal guilt had expired as political currency. Still, hitched to the broader despair of the Reagan years, Jackson was able to fashion a maverick candidacy. Crouch referred to Jackson as a "moral poet." Jackson's tremendous rhetorical gifts were never better displayed than at the convention podium that night in Atlanta.

> Providence has enabled our paths to intersect. [Dukakis's] foreparents came to America on immigrant ships; my foreparents came to America on slave ships.

But whatever the original ships, we're in the same boat tonight.

He crafted enduring metaphors: "That's the challenge to our party tonight, left wing, right wing—it takes two wings to fly," and "We are not judged by the bark we wear but by the fruit we bear." Grown men wept openly. In fairness, Jackson also had the freedom that comes with a symbolic campaign. His 1984 speech, for instance, did not contain a single reference to Walter Mondale, the party nominee.

But in 2004, during his convention speech, Obama was running for the Senate. The implications were immediately apparent. Obama opened by introducing himself and the route his father took to America. He described the country as "magical"—an adjective that his black critics would fixate upon as evidence of his unwillingness to challenge the country's racist traditions. Still, Obama's elegantly tailored and impeccably delivered speech introduced him to a national audience and began the "black president" buzz, which would surround him during his time in the Senate.

Both Jackson and Obama pleaded for unity—a requisite bit of convention boilerplate—but the parties they wanted to unite shed light on their differences. Jackson implored the Democratic Party to broaden its tent, to meaningfully include his "rainbow"—the poor, African Americans, gays, Latinos, and laborers—in its fold. By contrast, Obama spoke of a geographical, partisan divide.

> The pundits like to slice and dice our country into red
> states and blue states; red states for Republicans, blue
> states for Democrats. But I've got news for them, too.
> We worship an "awesome God" in the blue states, and
> we don't like federal agents poking around in our li-
> braries in the red states. We coach Little League in
> the blue states, and yes, we've got some gay friends in the
> red states. There are patriots who opposed the war in

Iraq, and there are patriots who supported the war in
Iraq. We are one people, all of us pledging allegiance to
the stars and stripes, all of us defending the United
States of America.

Jackson told of the United States he had seen during his months
on the campaign trail; Obama spoke of the America he hoped to
see when he set out on it. The lines of division are horizontal in
Jackson's appeal to unity, vertical in Obama's. How that would
translate into Obama's political priorities remained to be seen,
but the speech absolutely yielded great insight into how he
would campaign for the presidency.

IN THE SPRING OF 2008 *Time* magazine ran a cover story on vaccines. Increasing numbers of parents were opting out of the
shots, and the once-fringe anti-immunization movement was
poised to move into the mainstream. One researcher pointed to
a paradox: Vaccines had been so successful that a generation of
American parents grew up with no firsthand reference for the
painfully contorted limbs that polio wrought or the host of
other illnesses that once routinely claimed children's lives. The
result was that those who had most benefited from the advent of
vaccination were least equipped to appreciate the contribution.

On some level, Jackson appears to be driven by the concern
that the generation that has never seen a COLORED ONLY sign
outside a museum cannot recognize the weight of his generation's achievements. In some nearby tomorrow a young African
American may wonder whether a civil rights movement was ever
necessary—and whether black leaders are presently needed. Perhaps that concern will be valid fifty years in the future. For now,
though, it is apparent that the country's racial advances have not
obliterated racism and that the contributions of King and company did not diminish racism to some single strain kept locked
away from the public and studied as an artifact of history.

Several weeks after his comments became public, Jackson

gave a more contrite public address in which he plumbed the depths of his spirit and confessed the wrongfulness of the castration comments. The speech barely registered a blip on the media radar screen. Speaking in a cameraless room was a particular kind of purgatory for Jackson. But it did recall that other moment of contrition, the one in 1984 when Jackson's star was still ascending.

> If, in my low moments, in word, deed or attitude, through some error of temper, taste, or tone, I have caused anyone discomfort, created pain, or revived someone's fears, that was not my truest self. If there were occasions when my grape turned into a raisin and my joy bell lost its resonance, please forgive me. Charge it to my head and not to my heart. My head— so limited in its finitude; my heart, which is boundless in its love for the human family. I am not a perfect servant. I am a public servant doing my best against the odds. As I develop and serve, be patient: God is not finished with me yet.[29]

The alchemy of American politics cannot transform lead into gold, but we've become old hands at the opposite transformation. In telling the stories of men who are ahead of their time, we seldom note those graceless parts where the times catch up and pass them by.

CHAPTER 4

The Black Machine

THE OLD GUARD AND THE AGE OF OBAMA

IN 1931 THE SATIRIST George Schuyler published a gem of sarcasm called *Black No More*. In it a black scientist invents a device that allows black people to become white. Legions of blacks sign up seeking to escape Jim Crow, earn a decent living, or simply expand their sexual options. In the ensuing chaos the black leaders organize an emergency meeting to combat the insidious plot, not out of racial pride but because their economic survival depends upon it. Schuyler's vision of postracial society was a comically monochrome one where paranoid "whites" anxiously try to confirm their racial identity and black leaders fear that the end of racism will leave them unemployed.

In January 2008 satire began, in some ways, to resemble prophecy. The identity of 36 million African Americans remained unchanged, but racial progress began to resemble a threat to established black leadership. Five days into the new year Barack Obama won a presidential primary in a state with less than 5 percent black population—an unquestionable turning point in the history of American race relations. He followed the Iowa caucuses with a drumroll of victories in other white-majority states, racking up some fifteen wins by Super Tuesday. But amid the head-spinning developments that brought an

African-American candidate closer to the presidency than most of us had dared to imagine possible, we were missing one major implication: Barack Obama's candidacy signaled the death knell for the black civil rights leadership, or at least the illusion of their influence.

The most amazing development of the election cycle was not that a black candidate became a viable contender for the presidency, but that he received virtually no support from the civil-rights-era leaders whose sacrifices made his campaign possible. Black America's "greatest generation" had made their momentous achievements in creating a new social landscape, but as the Iowa returns rolled in, their leadership mandate expired dramatically.

In some ways black leadership is the last of the ethnic political machines. Across American history, political machines came into existence whenever a new group entered the political process. The nineteenth-century migrants pouring onto American shores generated fertile opportunities for ethnic patronage. Hence the Irish machines that populated New York and Boston for nearly half a century. A machine takes in raw aspiration and ethnic allegiance on one side and produces a reliable electoral result on the other. It dispenses patronage and affirms the power of the group amid a hostile pool of competitors.

African Americans, though, observed this process from the sidelines. For decades after the Fifteenth and Nineteenth amendments enfranchised them, local law and brutal custom made voting an exercise in jeopardy. The struggles of the civil rights era yielded not only a new black political leadership but millions of new black voters upon whom they could rely much as Irish, Italians, and Jews had done in the previous era. And at some point this arrangement came to loosely resemble a black machine, one that could parlay racial credibility into support for a chosen establishment candidate. This is something of a simplification, but not by much. In 1972, when Shirley Chisholm ran for president, the newly formed Congressional Black Caucus, of which she was a member, declined to endorse her. As the primary season wore on, Chisholm's quixotic quest for the White House came under active fire from her CBC colleagues.

The issue was not so much whom they chose to endorse as their reasons for doing so. Seven years after the passage of the Voting Rights Act the political power of black America had spilled far beyond its previous bounds, but the leadership's real authority lay in its ability to direct black voters toward their own white political patrons. That strategy reached its highest embodiment during the Clinton years, when the administration counted among its number the prominently placed blacks Mike Espy, Ron Brown, Alexis Herman, Joycelyn Elders, and Hazel O'Leary. Beneath them a second tier of black congressional figures parlayed their support for the "black" president into tangible yields. During the 2008 primary Congresswoman Maxine Waters of California, for instance, frequently referred to the fact that Bill Clinton had allocated the first funding for anti-HIV campaigns specifically targeting the black community.

On some level this ability to extract concessions was a mark of political maturity. But it operated on the tacit assumption that the most any black leader could aspire to was influence over more powerful white ones. It seemed to be a reasonable assumption, up until January 4, 2008.

Almost to a person, black leadership with civil rights credentials had lined up behind Hillary Clinton, for reasons ranging from personal benefit, to the complex relationship of the Clintons to black America, to political deal-brokering and patronage. But their tandem concern was to preserve their own political relevance. Then in district after district they proved unable to direct the black vote for Clinton. Thus at a moment when the hopes of the civil rights movement were most fully realized, when blacks and whites took a huge step toward a postracial future, the architects of that moment found themselves swept toward the periphery.

Positioned as he was between the black boomers and the hip-hop generation, Obama was indebted, but not beholden, to the civil rights gerontocracy. A successful Obama candidacy would simultaneously represent a huge leap forward for black America and the death knell for the civil-rights-era leadership—or at least for their business model.

An early example of the old guard's apparent aversion to Obama was a febrile YouTube rambling in which Andrew Young proclaimed Bill Clinton to be "every bit as black as Barack Obama" and offered armchair speculation that Clinton had probably bedded more black women during his lifetime than the senator from Illinois—as if racial identity could be transmitted like an STD. This might have been dismissed as a random instance of a politician speaking out of turn, were it not part of an ongoing pattern.

The previous spring Al Sharpton had cautioned Obama "not to take the black vote for granted," a statement of experience given that Sharpton had run for president in 2004 and received virtually none of it. Presumably he meant that the senator had not won over the supposed gatekeepers of the black electorate. Asked why he had not endorsed Obama, Sharpton replied that he would "not be cajoled or intimidated by any candidate."

Although Jesse Jackson was no stranger to Obama's situation—Coretta Scott King had endorsed Walter Mondale over him in 1984—he also got into the act. (It was at this point that he criticized Obama's response to the Jena Six case.) During one canvassing session an Obama supporter explained that generations of black politicians had operated with the understanding that the White House was permanently beyond their reach. But when a black man suddenly seemed to have a credible chance of winning, the logical question for those older politicians becomes, "Why not me?"

Even a broken clock is right twice a day, which explains the accuracy of Pat Buchanan's observation that "every great cause begins as a movement, becomes a business and eventually degenerates into a racket." Taken as a conglomerate, Jackson, Young, and Sharpton constituted a civil rights old-boy network that had parlayed its dated activist credentials into cash and jobs. Jackson leveraged his two presidential runs into a position as a CNN host. Young became mayor of Atlanta and U.S. ambassador to the United Nations. He then appeared to broker his moral credibility for ethically questionable causes: In the late 1990s he worked as a freelance consultant defending Nike against charges of using sweatshop labor in Asia. He sat on the board of Walmart, a business cited numerous times for low wages and antiunion activity, until (ironically) a racially insensitive statement forced him to resign.[30] In a similar vein Vernon Jordan, who had worked as a field director for the NAACP and served as executive director of the National Urban League, recast himself as a Beltway insider and political broker during the Clinton years.

To the extent that the term *leader* is applicable to these men, they likely represented the interests of Democratic Party insiders. Both Young and John Lewis endorsed Hillary Clinton; Sharpton and Jackson acted ambivalent, alternately mouthing niceties about Obama and criticizing his stances on black issues. There is far more to politics—even racial politics—than skin color, but it is nonetheless counterintuitive to think that Lewis, whose political career began when he was bludgeoned in Selma while fighting for black voting rights, witnessed the rise of the first viable black presidential candidate yet opted to support the Clinton machine.

Tellingly, in his YouTube commentary Young stated that he'd called his political connections in Chicago about Obama and been told "they don't know him." There are certainly valid reasons not to support one candidate or another, but absence of friends in common is a weak one. Young went on to announce that Obama was too young and should wait until 2016—a curious statement considering that Martin Luther King Jr., to whom Young was apprenticed, was just twenty-six when he launched the Montgomery bus boycott.

Until 2008, the influence of Al Sharpton and Jesse Jackson within black America remained unquestioned, and they, along with Andrew Young, John Lewis, and New York congressman Charles Rangel, were considered gatekeepers of the black vote.

But early in 2008 a divide that was largely, but not entirely, generational came to light. In South Carolina nearly all the black Democratic establishment lined up behind Hillary Clinton, but it had almost no ability to influence the black vote there. The truth is that while many white observers had long lamented the ubiquitous presence of Jackson and Sharpton as racial spokespersons, just as many African Americans were fatigued by their presence and looking for leadership alternatives. Our poll-driven, hyperanalyzed world provides nearly daily updates on the approval ratings for the president and Congress, but until the Obama campaign, information on black America's views of black leadership was virtually nil.

In a gesture of desperate futility, some of the old guard clung to the canard that Obama "isn't really black" and to its equally faulty sibling that Bill Clinton actually is "black." The argument was a thin shield against the charge that by supporting a white candidate—a Democratic machine candidate—the old guard was selling out the ideal of black advancement from which it had profited for decades.

Up to that point Obama had said comparatively little about the black planks in his platform—support for voter protection, employment assistance for ex-offenders, prenatal care for low-income mothers, ending sentencing disparities in the criminal justice system. His platform contained a comparatively strong set of civil rights priorities, but the campaign seemed more fixed on establishing who Obama was. In fact, his ability to win black voters' support depended on his ability to gain the support of white voters; and even with African Americans, his stances on big national questions took priority over his views on black-specific ones. The reality was that Obama was absolutely an African American, albeit in a way most people had not previously considered. His deficient "blackness" wasn't the biggest obstacle he faced in winning black voters, but within the mill of bar-stool punditry, it became the storyline of those first months.

In January 2007 Debra Dickerson grumbled about whites in-fatuated with Obama's embryonic candidacy:

> You're not embracing a black man, a descendant of slaves. You're *replacing* the black man with an immi-grant of recent African descent of whom you can ap-prove without feeling either guilty or frightened. If he were Ronald Washington from Detroit, even with the same résumé, he wouldn't be getting this kind of love . . . Since he had no part in our racial history, he's free of it . . . A non-black on the down low about his non-blackness is about to get what blacks have always asked for: to be judged on his merits. So let's pretend that we've really overcome.[31]

A few days later, with Obama still trailing Hillary Clinton in polls of black voters, the *New York Times* offered up an indo-lent piece under the banner "So Far Obama Can't Take Black Vote for Granted." The money quote was a confused offering from a fifty-eight-year-old African-American barber who remarked, "When you think of a president, you think of an American . . . We've been taught that a president should come from right here, born, raised, bred, fed in America. To go outside and bring some-body in from another nationality, now that doesn't feel right to some people."[32]

All along the notion that Obama lacked support because he wasn't a descendant of slaves simply didn't square with the numbers. In an Illinois senatorial debate against Obama in 2004, Alan Keyes tried that line of reasoning and saw himself nonetheless crushed among black voters—and every other kind of voter—on election day. Neither Al Sharpton, nor Carol Mose-ley Braun, nor Alan Keyes—all of whose ancestries were tied to American slavery—had done well with black voters when they ran for president. In 2004 Sharpton—whose ancestors were en-slaved by the ancestors of Senator Strom Thurmond—didn't even win the Washington, D.C., primary, where the population was nearly 60 percent black. Just a year earlier African-American voters had chosen white candidates over black ones in three major races: In the Ohio and Pennsylvania gubernatorial races, neither Ken Blackwell nor Lynn Swann received more than 20 percent of the black vote, and Michael Steele got only a quarter of the black vote in his Maryland Senate race. Their racial identities were never in question. Obama wasn't alone. No candidate—not even one whose race credentials were in good order—could take the black vote for granted. This fact worked to his favor. If African Americans were prepared to give a fair hearing to a white candidate who appealed to them, then they would certainly consider voting for a candidate who was black in a slightly different way.[33]

Wrongheaded as they were, those early questions helped shape Obama as a presidential candidate. In March he traveled to Selma to commemorate the 1965 voting rights march there. It was precisely the kind of gathering of civil rights era luminaries from which he had previously been notably absent. The speech he delivered that day was the first of the campaign's many brilliant moments. He responded to questions about his identity by placing himself directly in the lineage of the civil rights struggles.

> People been asking, "Well, you know, your father was from Africa, your mother, she's a white woman from Kansas. I'm not sure you have the same experience." And I tried to explain, "You don't understand. You see, my grandfather was a cook to the British in Kenya. Grew up in a small village, and all his life, that's all he was—a cook and a house boy." And that's what they called him, even when he was sixty years old. They called him a house boy. They wouldn't call him by his last name. Sound familiar?

The indignities of Jim Crow mirrored those of colonialism, and if Obama lacked a traditionally black American heritage, he had at least a close analogy. Then came as deft a statement as any he offered during the rest of the campaign, effectively recasting the civil rights movement as an act of global consequence and therefore one to which he was an heir.

> Something happened back here in Selma, Alabama. Something happened in Birmingham that sent out what Bobby Kennedy called "ripples of hope all around the world." Something happened when a bunch of women decided they were going to walk instead of ride the bus after a long day of doing somebody else's laundry. When men who had Ph.D.'s decided that's enough and we're going to stand up for our dignity. That sent a shout across oceans so that my grandfather began to imagine something different for his son. His son, who grew up herding goats in a small village in Africa, could suddenly set his sights a little higher and believe that maybe a black man in this world had a chance.
>
> This young man named Barack Obama got [a] ticket and came over to this country. He met this woman whose great great-great-great-grandfather had owned slaves; but she had a different idea, there's some good craziness going on. They decided that "we know that in the world as it has been, it might not be possible for us to get together and have a child, but something is stirring across the country because of what happened in Selma, Alabama, because some folks are willing to march across a bridge." So they got together, and Barack Obama Jr. was born. So don't tell me I don't have a claim on Selma, Alabama. Don't tell me I'm not coming home to Selma, Alabama.[34]

His knowledge of Selma's history was crucial for another reason: It brought him to the attention of Reverend Joseph Lowery, the aged firebrand and former lieutenant to Dr. King. Unlike many of his peers, Lowery held no elected office and was no longer the head of an institution. He was, in short, free, and he used that freedom to endorse Obama's fledgling campaign. The first time I saw Obama speak, in Atlanta two months after the campaign began, Joseph Lowery introduced him and provided the opening benediction. Coincidences in presidential politics are few, and the choice of Lowery to introduce Obama in the home of the civil rights movement was no accident. It was part of the campaign of subtleties meant to make the candidate more familiar, to connect him to black America's struggles. Obama had not come up through the civil rights establishment; he had kissed no black rings; the standard bearers of black leadership would not reliably vouch for him (which turned out to be an under-appreciated advantage). But an aged captain in those struggles offered a grandiloquent prayer on his behalf, and that certainly counted for something.

In the months after Selma, Obama deployed strategic sincer-ity in dealing with black voters. By turns and degrees his profes-sorial cadences acquired more gravy, his rhythms came to echo those of the black pulpit, and he ditched the occasional auxil-iary verb. In South Carolina he spoke to a black audience about Internet rumors warning them not to be *hoodwinked, bamboo-zled,* or *led astray,* and he brought the house down. Declaring that the civil rights movement influenced your life is one thing; quoting Malcolm X on the campaign trail is something entirely different. He told *Rolling Stone* magazine that Jay-Z and Ludacris were his favorite rappers. He showed up in a Marion, South Carolina, barbershop and immediately commenced trash-talking a patron's alligator shoes. It was a risky move, but his underlying point was to illustrate that he understood barbershop protocol. The campaign printed up posters of him sitting in that barber-shop and distributed the DVD of his visit.

During that spring I saw Obama speak to majority black crowds and majority white ones. He used two vastly differing styles. One was serious and professorial, with an unflappable un-dercurrent of cool; the other was loose-limbed and colloquial, yet with that same air of coolness. The question was not whether Obama was pandering—he absolutely was. The question was which audience he was pandering to. I saw that Obama was at least black enough to be bilingual in the way familiar to many other black professionals. He, like many of us, was fluent in the language of the soul food joint and in that of the country club. It was an ironic way of proving his black identity once again.

Another way was through his wife. Michelle Obama does not fit the standard dimensions of the American political wife. Independent with a sarcastic wit, serious and straight-talking—those are questionable virtues in that arena. But in opening doors within the black community, she was invaluable. The presence of a dark-skinned black woman, who was nearly six feet tall and who had earned substantially more money than he for most of their careers, made a case for the biracial son of an African immigrant with an unusual name. Early on, some media made fumbling efforts to cram her into a prefab box of black identity: Fox News derided her as a "baby-mama"; the *National Review* called her "Mrs. Grievance." To America at large, she was as unknown a quantity as her husband. But black people knew her. White campaign workers in South Carolina quickly learned that Michelle Obama could serve as an introduction, a voucher to black voters who had not seen anyone quite like her husband. They took his selection of a dark-complexioned woman as a sign of where his loyalties lay.

Michelle Obama remarked that the campaign was the first time in her adult life that she was really "proud" of this country. Media mercenaries howled, and reporters sifted through her college essays looking for traces of treason, but those were the most honest words spoken in 2008. In politics honesty is at times treated as a character flaw. The following day Cindy McCain, heiress and millionaire, offered a testimonial of her eternal pride in America. But thereafter people began referring to Michelle Obama as a potential liability to her husband's campaign. That line of thought found its ugliest incarnation in Juan Williams's hater-ish performance on Fox News just after the inauguration.

The new first lady was, he told viewers, "Stokely Carmichael in a ball gown." But in other arenas that ambivalence was an asset—it was a precise statement of sentiment that many black people felt during 2008.

Her critics tried to make Michelle Obama's ambivalence into a lack of patriotism, but it was precisely the opposite. Black patriotism is a faith born of Job: Its existence requires hope to constantly triumph over experience. It has triumphed with improbable frequency. Barack Obama's temperament and line of work prohibited him from saying these kinds of things. Unalloyed admiration for America is the default setting for any politician, particularly those seeking the presidency. Barack's disquieting experiences as a community organizer after college may have tempered his son-of-an-immigrant idealism, but you would never hear much about that from him, beyond the acceptable "we still have a lot of work to do" or "the playing field is not yet level."

His youthful wanderings led him to the South Side of Chicago, but Michelle Obama was born there. And randomly throughout the course of 2008, versions of Michelle Obama's remark were repeated. Middle-aged men and women registered to vote for the first time. Registered voters became first-time campaign contributors. Thousands trudged across counties, neighborhoods, and states to canvass for her husband. This was not unique to African Americans—the 2008 election brought millions of new voters to the polls, most of whom were not black. Had you asked them what their previous attitudes toward the nation's politics were, "really proud" would not likely have been among the responses. But Michelle Obama's statement echoed in a particular way within the black community: Barack was literally married to an experience that was as familiar as the South Side, Harlem, or Auburn Avenue.

These voters knew an Obama presidency would not mean the end of racism. But they also knew it would absolutely represent a fundamental change in the way this society understands race.

Younger Americans of all racial backgrounds recognized that fact more fully than their parents.

As polls showed increasing black support for Obama, Jackson, Sharpton, and Young began to look like a once-wealthy family that had lost its fortune but had to keep spending to maintain appearances. Obama's tepid showing among blacks in the early polls had more to do with name recognition and concerns about his viability as a candidate than with Jackson and Sharpton withholding their endorsement.

Ignoring Sharpton and Jackson was not the same thing as taking the black vote for granted. It was a reasonable calculation that neither of them could deliver enough votes to offset the number of white votes that their approval would have lost Obama.

In the days after Iowa the question of Obama's relationship to black America increasingly centered on the South Carolina primary, the first where black voters constituted a large part of the electorate. An Obama victory there would make it apparent that the black old-boy network was bouncing checks.

BLACK AMERICA IS not a democracy. Too much of its leadership is (self)-appointed and media-designated. Figureheads of all sorts derive their authority from the tagline beneath their names on CNN, but they are commonly associated with movements— "conservative spokesperson," "reproductive rights advocate"— rather than with entire ethnicities. The term *civil rights leader*, uttered with numb repetition, holds precisely no meaning at all. The issues confronting black America are vast, disparate, and complex, and many of them cannot be simply classified as violations of civil rights. At some point the term *civil rights leader* became a media cliché to describe black men who own bullhorns and/or speak in rhyming rhetorical flourishes. In October 2007, long before the Obama campaign, a writer in the *Washington Post* wondered why the media conferred the title "leader" on Al Sharpton when he served no discernible congregation, constituency, or community.[35]

Individuals who hold elective office are generally understood to represent their particular district or issue, but a motley lot of preachers, pundits, and prognosticators hold the at-large posts, and they are not accustomed to populist uprisings. Their business model is based upon their ability to reliably deliver black voters on behalf of those they support. Cable news hosts earn their paychecks by stoking the fires of the common man or woman on the Left or the Right. But black American has no equivalent figures charting the populist discontent of everyday people.

But for some time the "leaders" were showing signs of straying from their task. In the late 1990s Jesse Jackson's "Wall Street Crusade," an effort to increase the number of black financial services employees, and his effort to target NASCAR for, of all things, its lack of diversity inspired the view among some that he was little more than an ordained shakedown artist with a flair for rhyming phrases. In 2005 Al Sharpton shot a commercial endorsing LoanMax, a predatory lender that targeted minorities and charged up to 300 percent interest on its loans. In June 2008 Charles Steele, president of the Southern Christian Leadership Conference, which was founded by Dr. King, decried congressional efforts to regulate subprime credit cards—a financial hustle directed at poor minority communities. As an August 2008 report in *Mother Jones* revealed, the predatory loan industry had deep ties and even deeper pockets when it came to civil rights organizations. It was not surprising, then, that a July 2008 Gallup poll revealed a broad credibility gap between American blacks and their name-brand leadership. Asked whom they trusted to represent them on racial issues, respondents gave a double-digit endorsement to only a single African American: Barack Obama, who received 29 percent. Al Sharpton led the remainder with a feeble 6 percent, Jesse Jackson claimed only 4 percent, and beneath them were Maya Angelou, Oprah Winfrey, Colin Powell, Louis Farrakhan, and "my pastor," none of whom garnered more than 3 percent.[36]

On one level it could be read as a sign of maturity that the majority of black people did not place their faith in a single individual. On another it was a sign of discontent or even disillusionment with the state of black America and those who had led us there. But this discontent remained a hairline fault until Barack Obama's campaign began to gather momentum. Then it became a visible fracture and threatened to grow into an abyss.

Incumbency is the most powerful advantage that elected officials have. But members of the Congressional Black Caucus typically return to Congress more frequently and consistently than most other incumbents. One staffer phrased it bluntly: "If you are a black person in the House of Representatives, you are not supposed to ever lose an election."

The fact that only a handful of CBC incumbents have ever lost their seats has often benefited the districts they represent. When the Democratic Party achieved a congressional majority in the 2006 elections, black figures like Jim Clyburn, Charles Rangel, and Sheila Jackson Lee reached new levels of influence based upon their seniority. But that kind of job security lends itself to smug nonchalance. Edolphus Towns, the representative from New York's tenth district, is faithfully reelected despite having one of the worst attendance records in Congress. His record is not in degree or severity different from other congressional underachievement. But it starkly contradicts the moral weight of history and the blood sacrifices that were once required to ensure blacks access to the ballot.

All this lay inside the calculations to support Hillary Clinton. Few expected electoral consequences for endorsing someone other than the candidate their constituents favored. There were, of course, outliers. John Conyers, the twenty-term representative from Michigan, supported Obama, saying he would someday have to answer to his grandkids if he did otherwise. But in a sense those who supported Clinton were akin to those blacks who opposed the *Brown v. Board of Education* decision, many of whom had done years of service to the black community. They had principled reasons to be concerned about the Supreme

Court decision, ranging from concern for the future of black schools to contempt for the idea that black children needed the presence of whites in order to learn. But those nuances and subtleties tend to be lost to history, at least to the kind of conversational history that takes place at dinner tables and in barbershops. There they went down simply as having opposed the end of Jim Crow. On the most basic level, Clinton's black supporters would be derided as people opposed to the first black presidency.

In the political twilight zone of early 2008, there many plot twists. Stephanie Tubbs Jones, a revered congresswoman from Ohio, made the fatal error of acting as attack dog for the Clinton campaign—and was vigorously criticized by her constituents. Representative Sheila Jackson Lee supported Clinton—and was booed in her own district when she made a public appearance. Charles Rangel, chair of the House Ways and Means Committee and dean of New York's black politicians, endorsed his fellow New Yorker Hillary Clinton—but brushfires of Obama support broke out across his district.[37]

Post Iowa and New Hampshire, a narrative of dueling race and gender allegiances took hold in the media and pretty much everywhere else. Ahead of the second primary Gloria Steinem contributed an op-ed in the *New York Times* titled "Women Are Never Frontrunners." She saw Obama's victory over Clinton in Iowa as following a "historical pattern":

> Black men were given the vote a half-century before women of any race were allowed to mark a ballot, and generally have ascended to positions of power, from the military to the boardroom, before any women (with the possible exception of obedient family members in the latter).[38]

Steinem elasticized history to make the point: White women were not given the vote in 1870 precisely because of the number of female supporters of the Confederacy. Black male enfranchisement was not a token of racial advancement but part of a shrewd strategy to blunt the electoral authority of the former Confederates once they reentered the Union. In short, to have enfranchised white women in 1870 would have meant an immediate return to slavery for four million black men and women who still bitterly remembered the sting of the lash. But again, these were subtleties and nuances lost to our common understanding of the past.

What mattered was that if the Obama-Clinton duel was real, then black male leaders who supported Clinton could be charged with aligning themselves with whites over blacks, and black female leaders who supported her could be accused of prioritizing their gender over their race—an offense only slightly less heinous.

African Americans had many reasons to support Hillary Clinton, but Obama's failure to kiss rings or grease palms clearly gave her some advantages. His lack of obeisance to the established figures likely set some personality dynamics into motion that continued through the campaign season. His campaign's refusal to engage in retail politics created other discords. Ahead of the Georgia primary one municipal pol griped about the lack of funds coming down from the Obama camp and gleefully hissed, "The change Obama wants is not here yet."

Nor were political figures the only individuals invested in the old order. In December 2007 the conservative critic Shelby Steele rushed into print *A Bound Man*, a book bearing the unfortunate subtitle *Why We Are Excited About Obama and Why He Can't Win*. The author cobbled together a greatest-hits collection of racial clichés, none more threadbare than his observation that black voters would support only a racial firebrand or "prosecutor" (his terms), someone who would ceaselessly remind white America of its guilty inheritance of racism. Whites, on the other hand, would hew only to "bargainers" or smooth managerial types to whom blacks distrusted as traitors. Steele is a literary scholar, and his argument would have befit a novel (set in the 1960s) better than actual, three-dimensional reality. Reviewing the book in the *Nation*, blogger Ta-Nehisi Coates wrote:

> Intellectuals examining Obama are trapped in an ancient dynamic—one that even in its heyday was overstated—in which white and black America are constantly at each other's throats, and agree on nothing. The either/or fallacy is their default setting. ("Assimilation, not blackness, is the road to success," writes Steele.) They were made for a world where affirmative action and welfare reform were campaign issues, not one where universal healthcare and the Iraq War have dominated the debate.
>
> *A Bound Man* has the whiff of an author who spends very little time around the people he deigns to judge. The book misses the essential power of Barack Obama: that he is revealing for white America the quiet mass of black people who do not spend their days calculating the wages of slavery. Steele can't grasp that blackness, like any cultural force, works quietly and has no desire to be folded into square minds. Fortunately, it's people, not caricatures, who vote.[39]

Steele was no ward heeler collecting walking-around money, but his static conservatism was equally invested in race remaining anchored in a bygone era. The maddeningly obvious refutation of his pessimism lay in Reverend Lowery's statement—that blacks supported Obama after it became clear that he could win white votes—and in the fact that Obama's popularity with blacks rose in direct proportion to his popularity with whites. But no matter. There was more to come.

In an inscrutable act of bomb throwing, Bob Johnson, the founder of Black Entertainment Television, publicly highlighted Barack Obama's youthful dalliances with drugs. It was the mother of all pot-kettle situations. The statement, which prefaced a January 2008 television appearance by Clinton, was perplexing for multiple reasons, but especially because BET relied heavily upon an unceasing stream of hip gyrations, stereotypical images, and gymnastic booty shaking, which made Johnson a less than admired figure in some segments of the black community. As activist and radio host Davey D pointed out, Johnson's own network aired dozens of music videos in which rappers bragged about their drug dealing and drug consumption. His endorsement of Barack Obama might conceivably have cost the candidate votes, but his criticism only heightened Obama's standing. For weeks Johnson was on the receiving end of plantation-themed insults on blogs and talk radio.

Nor was Johnson the only member of the black media establishment to take aim at Barack Obama. Tavis Smiley, the host, commentator, and author, occupied a niche somewhere between journalism and advocacy. He functioned as a reporter and delivered op-eds on the nationally syndicated *Tom Joyner Morning Show*, but he also freely accepted endorsements and corporate contributions for his events that would have been outside traditional journalistic ethics. In the seven years since his acrimonious split with Johnson's BET network, Smiley had prospered.

Smiley's partnership with Joyner gave him access to the show's eight million weekly listeners and an additional 750,000 subscribers to the Web site. His PBS talk show provided an additional forum for his views. In 2000 he put his media access to use, organizing the first State of the Black Union, a brain trust of black politicians, activists, clergy, and intellectuals devoted to discussing the major concerns of the black community. Critics derided it as a talkathon, but the event often provided important perspectives on issues that went largely unmentioned in mainstream outlets. In 2007 Smiley extended an invitation to Barack Obama, who declined; the forum was scheduled for the same day as his campaign announcement. Smiley reportedly suggested that Obama make his announcement at the State of the Black Union, which Obama similarly declined.

In the ensuing days Obama came under fire from both Smiley and his close friend Cornel West. The criticism subsided over the year but re-emerged in 2008. Again Smiley extended an invitation, but this time the State of the Black Union conflicted with crucial campaign dates. Obama declined but offered to send Michelle in his place. Smiley replied tartly that Barack, not Michelle, was running for president. On the February 5 *Morning Show* Smiley threatened to reveal which candidate(s) had confirmed participation in the forum and which, in his estimation, were taking the black community for granted. He gave the candidates several days to comply before he would, in his words, "put them on blast" for their confused priorities.

The following week he revealed that Hillary Clinton would appear at the forum but Barack Obama would be absent. Many thought Smiley had overplayed his hand. Ignoring his program was not the same as ignoring the black community. Criticism poured into the radio station, with callers routinely asking if he was on the payroll of the Clinton campaign. Unsubstantiated rumors circulated that Smiley had made a deal to be Clinton's press secretary. Princeton political scientist Melissa Harris-Lacewell posted a scathing rejoinder on Theroot.com Web site titled "Who Died and Made Tavis King?"

> [Smiley] is mad because Obama has not promised to attend Smiley's "State of the Black Union" next week in New Orleans. At last year's SOTBU Al Sharpton, Cornel West and others joined Tavis in roundly criticizing Obama for not attending. Where was Barack that weekend? Oh yeah, he was announcing his bid for the U.S. presidency. This year, Obama is busy trying to win Texas, which has emerged as the firewall state for the Hillary Clinton campaign. Obama wins Texas; Hillary goes home. But Tavis & Co. think Obama should spend precious hours chatting with them about their agenda?[40]

Jack White, another Theroot.com contributor, ridiculed Tavis's attempt to issue a "black unity subpeona" to Obama, while CNN commentator Roland Martin firmly argued that going to New Orleans would be a strategic blunder for the campaign. Smiley began to look like another defrocked gatekeeper of the black vote and faced a cascade of listener criticism. In April, Smiley announced that he would leave the *Tom Joyner Morning Show*.

But while Obama did not attend, other notable black politicians did. Stephanie Tubbs Jones, bruised by the criticism of her support for Clinton and looking vulnerable after 70 percent of her district voted for Obama, showed up at the State of the Black Union bearing an olive branch. Sheila Jackson Lee, who saw 59 percent of her constituents go for Obama, appeared and highlighted her years of service to the black community. In an ironic twist Obama no longer needed their endorsement, but they could certainly have used his.

This thicket of contempt and confusion was the yield of South Carolina. Prior to its primary Obama was still a racial curiosity, an individual whose appeal to whites, it could still be argued, said nothing about his capacity to win over blacks. At that point, he could only have hoped that Shelby Steele had it half wrong.

SOUTH CAROLINA HAS AN ASTERISK that dictated the course of its history: It was the only colony where blacks formed the majority of the population. It began as the colony of a colony, intended to produce foodstock and supplies for the British sugar-producing plantations in Barbados. But the low-lying coastal regions were havens of malaria and disease. Successive attempts to cultivate the land failed, until enterprising colonists struck upon the idea of growing rice. Then came the import of Africans from the rice-growing regions along the western coast. Rice became profitable, and the number of hostage black workers swelled. By the late eighteenth century they outnumbered whites in the colony, creating a climate of paranoia and constant fear of slave revolt. Many began to see South Carolina as something of a Negro country in North America. On the coastal islands Africans' numbers were large enough to naturalize their own accents. The Gullah culture retained vast swaths of African tradition, secured by the fact that they were the numerically dominant population.

History came full circle in 2008. Blacks were no longer the majority of the state population, but they represented 29 percent, and they were 55 percent of the voters in the Democratic primary. Obama angled his campaign toward that bloc. He could run no postracial candidacy in South Carolina; he gleefully (and pragmatically) displayed every element of cultural affinity at his disposal. In December 2007 he deployed Oprah to warm up the crowd in Columbia. When addressing them, he fell into the black preacher cadences that had debuted in Selma nine months earlier.

The campaign staffers seized upon his intangible assets. When they realized that some black voters did not know he was African American, they ditched his old HOPE and CHANGE materials in favor of new literature with his picture prominently placed. White campaign staffers unfamiliar with the black community's pigment politics learned that Michelle Obama's dark complexion was an unstated benefit. For some, her color heralded an affinity with Marcus Garvey's revered "Black is Beautiful" campaigns of the 1920s, and the idea that proximity to whiteness was not the aesthetic standard for black America. While other regions of white America struggled clumsily to find language to categorize Michelle Obama—and fell back upon ill-fitting clichés like "baby-mama" and "radical militant"—she was infinitely familiar to black communities in South Carolina. So much so that she could be used to vouch for a man whose biracial heritage and exotic upbringing made him black in a new way.

The affectionate relationship between the couple resonated deeply with black voters. Indeed, the idealized family is a staple of American politics. Al Gore benefited from public displays of affection for his wife Tipper, particularly in the wake of Bill Clinton's public disgrace for philandering. John Edwards distinguished himself from the pack of presidential contenders partly because of his outward devotion to his ailing wife Elizabeth. (Only later did it become known that his "Two Americas" campaign apparently meant having a woman in each.) But something of another magnitude was at work in the way people saw and understood Barack and Michelle Obama. It was partly sociological, partly historical, and deeply personal.

The decline of the American family has been widely studied for decades, and no particular set of people is designated to shoulder its burden. But among black people every failed relationship becomes statistical grist, a data point in a broader indictment, to be examined in excruciatingly public detail. In America at large broken families are not autopsied; in black America they are given open-casket scrutiny. In that context the Obamas appeared to represent a mythical ideal of "black love," one that has been a mainstay of magazines like *Essence* and *Ebony* and the ballast of Afrocentric poetry for ages. It was most immediately visible after the two shared dap in Minnesota, after Obama formally won the Democratic nomination. I saw that brief meeting of fists at a campaign event surrounded by an overwhelmingly African-American crowd. The gesture registered with them immediately—they needed no pop culture interpreter to explain its meaning. It said to those arrayed around a massive flatscreen—and those watching around the world— that Michelle Obama was not only his wife but also his teammate and collaborator, his homegirl. Afterward it was subjected to an agonizing death by overanalysis. Yet as early as South Carolina black people understood a relationship universally regarded as awww-inducing almost as an act of fierce will and statistical defiance. Obama in South Carolina was channeling more African-American references than Black History Month in Harlem.

But beneath the soul campaign some serious political knives

were being thrown. The downsides to being a black presidential candidate were present not just among white voters. Reverend Joseph Lowery, the lieutenant to Dr. King who endorsed Obama and began traveling with him in the spring of 2007, stated it with his typical candor: "Black people are not interested in any more symbolic candidacies." All previous black presidential candidates had been tilting at electoral windmills. Under some circumstances—Jesse Jackson in 1988, for instance—black voters chose to become party to the implausible dream, if only to make a point. That second Jackson run paid huge dividends for black America, even as it fell short of Pennsylvania Avenue. But black voters had either ignored or dismissed the subsequent candidates—Carol Moseley Braun, Alan Keyes, Al Sharpton. Evidently symbolism was fine in 1988, but they were now look- ing for a candidate who might have a shot at actually addressing their needs. And that required that the candidate be—in that most threadworn term of punditry—"electable." Looking at South Carolina, Lowery simply said aloud what everyone else already knew: that Obama's ability to get black votes was teth- ered to his skill at attracting white ones. Given the fact that Obama and Clinton had split the two opening primaries, South Carolina was not simply a primary—it was a litmus test.[41]

In the months leading up to the South Carolina primary, the Clinton campaign invested heavily in the state. Bill Clinton's long-standing ties to the black political establishment, combined with the deep pockets of Hillary's campaign, ensured that Clinton would sew up the endorsements of the major state and municipal officials—and therefore the black vote—long be- fore the polls opened. This is how it had always been done, in the four decades since the passage of the 1965 Voting Rights Act: Black politicians and pastors functioned as de facto gatekeepers of the black vote. In some instances the line between endorsing and delivering blurred. State Senator Darrell Jackson, for in- stance, also served as pastor of an eleven-thousand-member church. During the 2004 presidential season he signed on as a consultant to John Edwards's campaign, for a $15,000 monthly fee. His influence helped deliver the state to Edwards, despite the candidate's previous losses in Iowa and New Hampshire. That kind of operation was replicated across the state: A shepherd in each precinct was designated to deliver black votes, and in the weeks approaching election day, more cash would be allocated as walking-around money—funds used to hire canvassers, drivers, and unspecified fixers who could guarantee voter turnout. Depending upon where you stood, this was either crass retail politics or a means by which underserved communities found alternative sources of funding.[42]

The Obama campaign recognized this dynamic early on and took the unconventional step of hiring as state political director a community organizer with limited political experience. Anton Gunn picked up *The Audacity of Hope* in an airport concourse in 2006 and became so engrossed, he missed his flight. He met then-Senator Obama at a book signing and told him if he ever ran for president, he wanted to work for the campaign. Both men had organized for the Gamaliel Foundation after college and quickly fell into a dialogue about their shared experiences as community activists. After Obama announced his candidacy, Gunn thought he might land a position coordinating volunteers or directing a campaign office. Instead Obama's staff contacted him and said he would be running the primary campaign in South Carolina. The full task they assigned him was even more daunting: He was to create a parallel structure that could bypass the state's patronage system. He was to take the case for Barack Obama directly to the people of South Carolina.[43]

Gunn is a massive, charismatic community organizer who, at thirty-four, still looked every bit the offensive lineman he had been at the University of South Carolina. Aside from a failed bid for the state legislature, the sum of his political involvement was directing a nonprofit called Fair Share that supported social justice issues for impoverished communities. For the Obama campaign, he fell back upon his two areas of expertise: community organizing and selling Amway. He treated the candidate like a multilevel marketing product, creating a DVD about the platform and cultivating a cadre of people who would invite "someone from work, someone from church and someone from their family" to their homes to watch it. There would be no walking-around money, no oily consultants extracting exorbitant fees for ambiguous services. He had his own grievances with the old order, and "this was an opportunity . . . for me to invest in a leadership change in South Carolina—not the old, heavy-handed preacher-politician type that every presidential campaign buys off with some money in the offering plate and a bucket of chicken."

He kept track of the watch parties and their generations—the friends of friends of friends of the original group. On the ground the Obama campaign looked like a cross between a grassroots movement and a pyramid scheme. It kept growing. The clash between the Clinton campaign's approach to black voters and that of the Obama campaign became apparent early on. State legislators awaited visits from Gunn and the harvest of funds that he would arrange in exchange for their endorsement. The campaign politely allowed them to continue hoping, but the visits never materialized. One official approached the campaign requesting a $5,000 payment up front and a $3,500 monthly retainer in exchange for the public relations value of him "telling everyone I support you" and putting some people on the street during the vote. Gunn thanked him for his proposal and said he would get back to him—placing him in a growing pool of Carolina pols left sitting futilely by the phone.

By the summer of 2007 Gunn wanted to be seen anywhere except the grounds of the state capitol. Hillary Clinton's operatives were dropping money onto the street, and the Obama team sought to avoid a bidding war for legislators' support. Still the cash flowed freely—the Clinton camp reportedly dropped $300,000 in a single South Carolina district. In the fall of 2007 South Carolina gradually became a microcosm of black leadership nationally. Blacks, after being barred from contention for aeons, after a history defined by disfranchisement and the lynching of voters, had finally found a place at the table. No matter that the cards were being dealt from the bottom of the deck, or that many of them were more committed to bank accounts than to accountability. On the basic epidermal level there was awkward triumph in the fact that white politicians were now forced to sweat dollars if they wanted black support. But life is not lived on the basic epidermal level. "Every time a presidential campaign comes to town, someone gets a big check, but all he does is give out a little gas money and buy a little food," Gunn told me. "Most of that money never really gets to the congregations or even the community. That is something I've seen." The problem was that a system that had previously worked for none had been replaced by one that worked for the few. Gunn was hoping for a new one that could work for the many.

As with much else, this conflict took on generational hues. The Obama side took to approaching elected officials who were under forty and hopefully less steeped in the traditional ways of doing business. In exchange for the officials' allegiance, the campaign offered only the currency of appreciation. The *Wall Street Journal* reported a story about a sixty-three-year-old black councilwoman and ardent Clinton supporter trying to fend off the inroads that a twenty-two-year-old black Obama organizer was making in her home district.[44]

In truth, there was more to the story than price tags and receipts. Nationally many of the black leaders who lined up behind Clinton had spent years if not decades accruing a balance of favors. For some, Clinton's campaign represented a last chance for them to cash in on a career of carefully cultivated alliances, favors, and influence. A quid pro quo this time might actually translate into benefit for their districts, constituents, and communities. Representative Maxine Waters repeatedly pointed to the Clinton era's anti-HIV funding as evidence that the Clintons could be trusted to do right by black America. By contrast Obama, to many involved, was an unknown quantity.

To an amazing degree, candidate Obama and the old guard

were simply unfamiliar with each other. Echoing Andrew Young's earlier comment, Maxine Waters said of her fellow Congressional Black Caucus member:

> I didn't know him. Most of us didn't know him. I'm told we may have been in some of the same venues in past years, but I never actually met him. Clinton, I had known and worked with for years.[45]

For Obama's part, the young, largely white Ivy Leaguers upon whom his campaign relied did not know the geography of the black community. Their reportedly brusque handling of Waters, highly respected among blacks, did not make it easy for them to find inroads. Eric Easter had been the press secretary for Jesse Jackson's campaign and was now chief of digital strategy for Johnson Publishing. When he published a mildly critical piece on Obama, he received a terse phone call from a publicity person affiliated with the campaign. Easter asked the flack how he expected to do PR for a black presidential candidate and not even know he was talking to the person who had run PR for the last major black candidate. In another story a reporter interviewing Barack Obama caught an exchange on tape in which the senator dismissed a Congressional Black Caucus meeting in order to continue the interview. It worked in his favor with the journalist but certainly not with the CBC.

Rapid change brings with it a loss of institutional memory. In one of the more severe stretches of the Jeremiah Wright fiasco, one observer pointed out that a closer relationship with the old guard might have served Obama well. At the very least one of Wright's peers might have cajoled him into avoiding more press exposure. But all this had yet to be seen.

This concern developed throughout the late fall and into the winter of 2007, then accelerated after the stunning Iowa victory. In mid-January the campaign began sending massive caravans of volunteers into the state from North Carolina and Georgia. The headquarters in Columbia hung banners welcoming volunteers who drove to the state directly from New Hampshire. At some moments the volunteer-departure points in Atlanta resembled the staging grounds for the Normandy invasion—one Saturday a single office in the city provided twenty-six van loads of volunteers.

Early on primary day, January 26, the arteries leading out of Georgia were fairly congested with vehicles plastered with campaign bumper stickers and HOPE placards taped onto doors. One team spent twelve hours scouring tiny Denmark, South Carolina, for voters, fearful that a low turnout in the town would be indicative of a poor statewide performance and, with nearly every canvasser's cell phone battery dead, lapsed into a news blackout.

The initial returns in South Carolina, delivered to them by hearsay and secondhand reports, were not to be believed. Obama had won by 28 points; he took a massive 80 percent of the historic large black vote. In district after district, community after community, the pastors and politicians had proved utterly incapable of directing the black vote to their patrons. South Carolina was a rejection not simply of Clinton as a candidate but of an entire way of doing business. In the wake of the blowout Bill Clinton commented to a reporter that Jesse Jackson had also won South Carolina. The clip went radioactive. To a large portion of the black audience, the words diminished the accomplishment of one black candidate by placing him in the same category as another losing candidate who had had nothing in common with him beyond race. John Edwards had also won South Carolina (more recently than Jackson) but failed to ultimately win the nomination. Why then the Jesse comparison?

Whether the comment was meant to be innocuous or belittling, Clinton was the white man in America least capable of claiming he didn't know how a statement would go over with a black crowd. Parlor talk turned to revoking Clinton's Honorary Black Man title. A UPS delivery man arrived at my door the following week, glimpsed the Obama sign in my window, and said, "Those Clintons sure showed us their true colors," before dropping off the package.

Clinton had torn his pants badly. Dr. Johnetta Cole, the president of Bennett College, a historically black college for women in North Carolina, had deeper ties to the former president than most. She and Hillary Clinton shared a common friend in Marian Wright Edelman, founder of the Children's Defense Fund. During his tenure in the White House, Bill Clinton had considered appointing Cole secretary of education. After he left office, he came to the aid of the college, organizing a dialogue with Bob Dole on campus that raised $2 million at a crucial time. Yet during the primaries she found herself leaning toward Barack Obama and after South Carolina committed to supporting him.

> It's been, at times, a very disturbing journey for me. Hillary Clinton had come to Spelman at my invitation; I'd served on Bill Clinton's transition team. And so it was, without even a lot of conscious thought, I would support Hillary Clinton. But as I began to watch the campaign, my disappointment really grew. And by the time we got to South Carolina, I would say it was not only disappointment but it was hurt. I saw a campaign driven by a notion of inevitable victory, of entitlement to a post and carelessness around questions of race that said to me "This is really not good."[46]

But in the midst of the uproar over his comment, one key fact was overlooked by most, including Clinton. Jackson and Obama had won South Carolina in radically different ways. Both had relied heavily upon the black vote, but Jackson had succeeded despite that fact that he could not win a general election; Obama had won precisely because he could.

In the following weeks African Americans commonly referred to the Clintons disparagingly as "good white folks." The term harked back to the dark days of Jim Crow, when most blacks found their employ providing services for white families. Conventional wisdom held that there were bad white folks, who deeply imbibed and exhibited the doctrine of white superiority, and there were good white folks, who displayed a kind of ASPCA liberalism in dealing with Negroes. It was the difference between being ordered to a task with the threat of violence and being requested to do it—you still had no real option of refusing. Neither believed in racial equality, but the latter allowed a small shred of dignity to remain intact. This was an overstated comparison, but beginning in South Carolina and in subsequent appearances, Bill Clinton seemed determined to prove it to be apt.

In so doing he not only made life harder for the black politicians who were supporting his wife's presidential ambitions but also made propping up the black machines more difficult. The flaws of the old way had become increasingly apparent, but Clinton's remark ensured that its implicit paternalism and condescension would also be placed in public view.

Political machines, like the humans they serve, are inescapably bound to a life cycle. They are created, mature, and ultimately fall away against a tide of change. The old American machines, based upon ethnic loyalty, fell apart because of corruption and because the needs of the group they represented became more complex. It is one thing to dictate the behavior of all the Irish living on the Lower East Side, but quite another to do so for subsequent generations in far-flung suburbs who have vastly different relationships to taxes, education, and the very idea of citizenship.

The night Obama won Iowa, Baratunde Thurston had informed Jesse Jackson that black interests were far more diverse than they had ever been and that he was as likely to vote on the basis of the Iraq War as on any race-specific issue. It was a classic encapsulation of the civil rights and post–civil-rights generations. The machines and the many-varied thing that comes in its wake.

The opening months of 2008 unveiled another irony. For generations the prerequisite for a black entering an institution for the first time was proving that they were just like the establishment that ran it. Jackie Robinson's temperament and college education were as important as his athletic talent when the

Dodgers chose him to integrate baseball. Sidney Poitier rose through the tiers of Hollywood with his nimble mastery of an archetype: the intelligent, articulate, and polished Negro.

Obama's smooth demeanor and even temperament reminded many of Poitier, but the resemblance was superficial. While his predecessors had struggled to prove themselves worthy of insider status, Obama became vastly successful by doing just the opposite: masterfully positioning himself as an outsider. In rejecting the old ways, he necessarily blew off a portion of that history and that struggle. It was collateral damage of change.

All this was yet to be digested on January 26, as tens of thousands of volunteers from around South Carolina converged upon the capital and the convention center, where their candidate would speak. Parking decks overflowed, and people jammed the center to capacity. Outside, jubilation was rising. Inside, the candidate told the throng and the thousands crowding the streets and the hotel lobbies nearby:

> The choice in this election is not about regions or religions or genders . . . It's not about rich versus poor, young versus old, and it's not about black versus white. This election is about the past versus the future.[47]

He was right, but his message was joyously lost on at least one reveler. Outside the convention center a slender, light-brown-complexioned woman adorned in a pillbox hat, pearls, horn-rimmed glasses, and clothes from the 1950s held a sign that made people stop and point. She conjured the image of that revered icon of the Montgomery bus boycott. The sign read ROSA PARKS LOVES BARACK.

CHAPTER 5

The Joshua Generation

THE AGE DIVIDE AND OBAMA

IT WAS JANUARY 20, and a pretty woman with brown skin stood on Auburn Avenue, her arms wrapped in a self-hug as she shivered against the cold. She wore shoes completely impractical for standing in the twenty-degree Atlanta weather, and she danced up and down occasionally to keep the blood circulating. She wasn't alone; hundreds of others were improvising their own strategies to keep warm as they kept their eyes fixed on a massive screen. Just to her right was the newly built crypt where Coretta Scott King's remains rested next to those of her husband, Dr. Martin Luther King Jr. In fact, the last time Auburn Avenue saw lines like these was two days after Mrs. King's death, when mourners stood outside for hours for a chance to pay homage to her and Martin's shared dream.

But this time they were gathered in the hope of seeing Barack Obama speak at Ebenezer Baptist Church's annual Martin Luther King Day service, even if that meant watching it on the massive overflow screen on the church's front lawn. "Forty years have gone by since Dr. King's death," said Reverend Raphael Warnock, 38, pastor of Ebenezer Baptist. "In biblical terms, the number forty holds powerful symbolism." He let the words hang.

The Ebenezer faithful know that forty is the number of days

God unleashed the fury waters of the Old Testament; the age of the prophet Muhammad when the Koran was revealed to him; the number of years that the children of Israel wandered before entering the Promised Land. It was also the number of years between the death of Martin Luther King and the day Barack Obama stood in the sanctuary of King's church as the frontrunner for the Democratic presidential nomination.

"The generation that left bondage in Egypt wandered for four decades," Reverend Warnock said, building toward his point, "but it was their *children* who were the first to enter the Promised Land."

Warnock's graceful pulpit manifesto was not lost on the congregation. Standing in King's church next to Barack Obama, he'd offered a subtle jab at the civil-rights-generation leaders—including Andrew Young—who had overwhelmingly lined up behind Hillary Clinton, offering an explanation for why so many young black Obama supporters had begun referring to those born after Dr. King's death as "the Joshua Generation."

Eight hundred miles away a separate drama was unfolding. Reverend Calvin Butts, pastor of Harlem's influential Abyssinian Baptist Church, was a committed Hillary Clinton supporter. He was also Warnock's mentor. On some level his support for the Clintons was understandable—Bill Clinton's offices were only a few blocks away on 125th street. Hillary Clinton represented his state in the U.S. Senate. And Butts had long been a political insider, forging close connections that benefited the church's educational and community development efforts. But on another level, the pastor was exhibit A in the case against the black leaders so indebted to white Democrats that they were unable to support a history-defining black candidacy. Only a day earlier Butts had formally endorsed Clinton and invited her to speak at the church; the move generated a wave of dissent among the congregation. Rightfully or not, Butts's endorsement of Clinton and Warnock's all-but-endorsement of Obama in the same week looked like a neat metaphor for the generational divide in black America. On one level, that divide was really no different from any other rift between age groups. But to view the struggle for equality through a generational lens was part of a cycle unique to African Americans.

In the early days of Emancipation, ex-slaves rejoiced in the growth of the "freeborns," the generation that was born outside slavery. At the same time Frederick Douglass, Harriet Tubman, Sojourner Truth, Booker T. Washington, and others derived a portion of their authority from the fact that they had survived that brutal institution. The first generation of northern-born blacks bore a different relationship to the world than their southern-bred kin. Their lack of deference to whites and their expanded menu of life possibilities were viewed as progress, but their parents lamented that they might lose the connection to the traditions that had brought them thus far on the journey.

The civil rights generation had to combat their parents' doubts and opposition in order to seize their own moment in history. Martin Luther King Jr. was sharply and frequently criticized by the old guard of his own Baptist denomination, and the older leadership of the NAACP harbored a low-grade hostility toward the young preacher and his new methods. The twenty-six-year-old King led the Montgomery bus boycott over the protests of his own father and Benjamin Mays, a college mentor whom King Sr. had enlisted in an attempt to talk him out of the effort. And now in Ebenezer Baptist Church another young preacher was speaking on behalf of a generation born under novel circumstances: outside the system of segregation and restriction that, in one way or another, had been the backdrop for the entirety of black history in America.

Ironically, a civil rights generation best known for its idealism was cynical about Obama's prospects. Yet Obama was indebted to his activist predecessors, and not just because they opened doors and blazed trails. His debt was direct, profound, and enduring in both personal and political terms.

Throughout the spring Obama's literature consistently refer-enced an axiom of the campaign: "I'm asking you to believe. Not just in my ability to bring about real change in Washington . . . I'm asking you to believe in yours." He was commonly hailed as a candidate who could move beyond the old axes of American politics, the aged holdovers from 1960s culture wars that he dis-missed as "psychobabble" in the pages of *The Audacity of Hope*. But comments like that one, deflecting authority back onto the people at the grassroots, were derived from those very struggles. Look at the campaign's ground-up leadership style, and it was impossible not to think of Students for a Democratic Society and their 1960s campaigns for participatory democracy. Or SNCC's Freedom Summer and Mississippi Freedom Democratic Party initiatives. To the extent that he was competing for the black vote, or that there even was a black vote to compete for, he owed former SNCC activists like Marian Wright Edelman and Con-gressman John Lewis, both of whom were, ironically, supporting Hillary Clinton.

In 1965, as the civil rights movement reached its zenith of in-fluence, Dr. King, SNCC, and the NAACP turned their attention toward the violent southern traditions that had effectively nulli-fied the Fifteenth and Nineteenth amendments, at least as they pertained to black people. The result was one of the more brutal episodes in the movement's history. Selma, Alabama police bludgeoned Lewis as they derailed an attempted march for vot-ing rights. Klansmen made the city ground zero in their efforts to stave off the tide of change. They deployed the customary tactics, attacking black civil rights workers; Viola Liuzzo, a white volunteer from Detroit, was murdered for her civil rights sympathies. And out of Bloody Sunday came a mandate for Lyndon B. Johnson to sign the Voting Rights Act, ensuring fed-eral protection for black voters. Not only did Obama owe his political career to their successes, but the circumstances of his birth were directly impacted by the NAACP lawyers and ac-tivists who supported the *Loving v. Virginia* case, which made interracial marriage legal across the nation.

One month after he was sworn in as a U.S. senator, Barack Obama spoke at a birthday gathering for John Lewis. The moral power of the movement, he said, had transformed places like Cairo, Illinois, once a stronghold of a white citizens' council, into a place where a black senatorial candidate could attract hundreds of supporters. He offered his forebears an homage:

> You know, two weeks after Bloody Sunday, when the [Selma] march finally reached Montgomery, Martin Luther King Jr. spoke to the crowd of thousands and said, "The arc of the moral universe is long, but it bends towards justice." He's right, but you know what? It doesn't bend on its own. It bends because we help it bend that way. Because people like John Lewis and Hosea Williams and Martin Luther King and Coretta Scott King and Rosa Parks and thousands of ordinary Americans with extraordinary courage have helped bend it that way. And as their examples call out to us from across the generations, we continue to progress as a people because they inspire us to take our own two hands and bend that arc.

Two years later, as his presidential campaign was fending off the silly canard that he might not be black enough, Obama returned to Selma and to that theme of indebtedness. But he added a new biblical theme. He told the audience:

> As great as Moses was, despite all that he did, leading a people out of bondage, he didn't cross over the river to see the Promised Land. God told him your job is done . . . We're going to leave it to the Joshua genera-tion to make sure it happens. There are still battles that need to be fought; some rivers that need to be crossed . . . The previous generation, the Moses gener-ation, pointed the way. They took us 90 percent of the way there. We still got that 10 percent in order to cross

over to the other side. So the question, I guess, that I
have today is, what's called of us in this Joshua generation? What do we do in order to fulfill that legacy, to
fulfill the obligations and the debt that we owe to those
who allowed us to be here today?

This was precisely the point. Obama attempted to honor those
elder statesmen of struggle, even as he nudged them into twilight. He delivered a brief for change in the mildest tones and
most complimentary language. Perhaps a portion was lost in
translation, or perhaps black leadership is no different from any
other group that gains a modicum of power. Frederick Douglass
once warned that "power concedes nothing without demand. It
never has and it never will." It was easy to overlook the fact that
Douglass's words are valid across racial lines.

OF ALL THE civil-rights-generation leaders, Obama's relationship with Lewis took on the starkest generational tones. The
congressman's political career was inextricably bound to that
Sunday in Selma, the struggle's Antietam. In 1986 Lewis was
elected to represent Georgia's fifth congressional district in a
campaign that pitted him against fellow civil rights veteran
Julian Bond. In subsequent years he became the point person
on the Voting Rights Act, shepherding it through Congress each
time portions of the bill went up for renewal. Yet in a district
where 74 percent of the voters supported Obama, Lewis pledged
his superdelegate support to Hillary Clinton—apparently con-
tradicting his years as an icon of black political empowerment.
Other constituents saw it in less racial terms: It was morally
wrong for a representative of the people to defy the will of his
own constituents in order to repay a political debt or earn bar-
gaining points with the Clintons.

The contrast was especially striking to one constituent in particular. Malaika Moses Mitchell, a graduate of Spelman College, had supported Obama since early in the campaign. Her

parents were also activists who worked with John Lewis during the SNCC days: Her father, Bob Moses, was the main organizer of the 1964 Freedom Summer Project, which registered hundreds of black voters and directly challenged disenfranchisement in Mississippi. Nearly forty-four years later, Mitchell initiated a voter petition to force Lewis to use his superdelegate vote to express the will of his district.

"Those of us in our twenties and thirties have different experiences from our elders and a different type of optimism," she told me. "A lot of them had that when they were our age, but through positions and titles, they've become part of mainstream politics and resistant to something new." Her petition spread rapidly throughout the Internet, garnering signatures from people across the country who saw Lewis's support for Clinton as something of a betrayal. In late February, under mounting pressure, Lewis switched his support to Obama. He explained his change of heart in civil rights terms: "I came to see that Barack's effort was a movement akin to what we were doing in the late 1950s and 1960s. I wanted to be on the right side of history."[48]

In truth, Lewis's early allegiance to Clinton was neither unique nor particularly egregious. It was, however, the action of someone who did not recognize the seismic undercurrents changing the country—even if he was partly responsible for creating them. The more cynical stances—Andrew Young's declaration that Bill Clinton and Barack Obama were equally black, and Bob Johnson's assault, for instance—were notable, but they weren't new. By 2008 Obama, in fact, was well acquainted with those kinds of charges.

In his 2004 race against Obama for the Illinois senate, Alan Keyes assaulted his rival for not being "black." Whether he was referring to Obama's mixed ancestry or to the fact that he did not descend from enslaved Africans, Keyes's racial excommunication had no effect—except that he suffered an almost unchristian beating at the polls, even among voters who met or exceeded his definition of *black*. Four years earlier, when Obama lost his bid to unseat Congressman Bobby Rush, the district line was that the incumbent was a representative of the black community while the upstart was a product and ally of the white barons at the University of Chicago. During the early presidential campaign, those claims took on self-serving importance. If Obama wasn't "really black," his critics could not be accused of "really selling out." Thus came the absurd reality that a black former civil rights attorney had to prove his allegiance to the black community.

Nor was Obama's experience unique. In 2002 Cory Booker, a thirty-two-year-old Newark city councilman, challenged the sitting mayor Sharpe James, in a race that turned into a trial balloon for generational politics. Booker is a Rhodes scholar and a Yale Law graduate. James's supporters assailed him with a chorus of jeers, rolling through the streets of Newark on a flatbed shouting, "You ain't black, you're suspect, boy!" Rumors circulated that Booker—both of whose parents are black—was actually biracial. In the midst of one debate James informed his opponent, "You have to learn to be black, and we don't have time to teach you." James was a case study in the ambivalent blessings of the post-civil-rights era. If the machine was the people, then the opponent of the machine was, by definition, an enemy of the people. Or at least a foreigner in their midst. If James was for us, who could be against us? It was a lithe sequence of cynicism and logic, an abracadabra to blur the lines distinguishing Sharpe James's interests from those of the People. And enough to deliver James another victory.[49]

In 1970, against a backdrop of historic corruption, mob influence, and disempowered black communities, Newark had elected its first black mayor. It was a signal achievement of the Black Power movement. But nearly forty years later the city's problems remained, only now a black official presided over them. It was a cynic's version of progress.

As black officials rose to power in other cities, the lines of allegiance and self-interest became hazy. At what point did voters making demands on city hall become a means to cripple black

leaders already hampered by white business and state government? Barack Obama encountered this dynamic years earlier
when he worked as a community organizer. A group of South
Side pastors stiff-armed his efforts to build a grassroots coalition. The presence of Harold Washington, a black man, in the
mayoral office meant that change had come. You had no need
to fight the power if the power looked like you. After Obama
pitched his community initiative to a group, one pastor took it
upon himself to educate the young idealist:

> The last thing we need is to join up with a bunch of
> white money and Catholic churches and Jewish organ-
> izers to solve our problems . . . White folks come in
> here thinking they know what's best for us, hiring a
> buncha high-talking college-educated brothers like
> yourself who don't know no better . . . Things have
> changed with our new mayor. I've known the district
> police commander since he was a beat cop. The alder-
> men in this area are all committed to black empower-
> ment. Why we need to be protesting and carrying on at
> our own people?[50]

James Baldwin once observed that bureaucracies cannot
comprehend human suffering, they can understand only threats
to their own continued existence. The myth of the postracial
politician begins with the knowledge that bureaucracy and ineptitude are color-blind. Leadership even of good conscience and
talent was constrained in just how much it could bring home to
its black constituents, as the trials of Harold Washington, Tom
Bradley, and Coleman Young illustrate. These kinds of experiences shaped Obama's later political views, but more important
they created common ground with the rising class of black public servants who, like him, had come of age confronting the
shortcomings of epidermal politics.

More than any of the African Americans who preceded them,

Obama and the politicians he is most frequently compared to—
Massachusetts governor Deval Patrick, Mayors Adrian Fenty of
Washington and Cory Booker of Newark (he ran again in 2006
and won), and to a lesser degree, former representative Harold
Ford and Mayors Shirley Franklin of Atlanta and Michael Nutter of Philadelphia—have a wide avenue toward leadership. The
earlier generation of leaders was a succession of clergymen who
solemnly prayed the race into a better day.

In 1944 Adam Clayton Powell Jr. used his position as pastor
of Abyssinian Baptist Church to launch a successful campaign
for a congressional seat, becoming the first black to represent
Harlem. That victory became the template for political success.
Powell's generation shared affiliations with historically black
colleges, fraternities, and sororities, but the church remained the
unquestioned launching pad for political aspirations. By contrast, none of the current figures commonly cited as "postracial"
have backgrounds in the clergy. Jesse Jackson and Sharpton are
reverends; Jackson and Andrew Young graduated from historically black North Carolina A&T and Dillard University, respectively. Jackson is a member of Omega Psi Phi fraternity, Young
of Alpha Phi Alpha, and Lewis of Phi Beta Sigma, all African-
American fraternities. But, Obama (Columbia and Harvard
Law), Patrick (Harvard and Harvard Law), Booker (Stanford,
Oxford, and Yale Law), and Nutter (University of Pennsylvania)
bypassed black educational institutions in favor of Ivy League
ones.

In the new era black leaders have emerged who have not been
shaped by any specifically black institution aside from their families. But this phenomenon should not be called "postracial."
Obama's community work introduced him to the stunted opportunities that still broke down along racial lines. Patrick spent
years as an attorney with the NAACP Legal Defense Fund fighting discriminatory practices that had survived the civil rights
movement like cockroaches in a nuclear winter. Booker, Nutter,
Franklin, and Fenty, as mayors of cities with sizable or majority
black populations, had to recognize the ways race infused the

needs and concerns of their citizens even without defining the entirety of their agenda.

If the new leaders were less prone to playing race card politics or using charges of racism to cloak their own character or political flaws, they were nonetheless operating in a context in which race mattered. As were their constituents. As was their country. In August 2008 the *New York Times Magazine* ran an article called "Is Obama the End of Black Politics?" that was almost transparent as wishful thinking. When the reporter asked Nutter about being postracial, he nearly laughed. Just prior to the Democratic Convention I posed the question to Shirley Franklin and she all but rolled her eyes before commenting that she was the mayor for all of Atlanta but her career began with the black community. In the mid-1990s the local Washington press began hailing Mayor Anthony Williams as "postracial," given that he did not excite the same polarizing passions as Marion Barry. But when the biracial Fenty assumed office in 2007, he was hailed as even "postracial-er." A skeptic might make something of a fact that the politicians deemed postracial were almost always light-complexioned. In the end, the label seemed no more than an awkward designation for those blacks who eat Brie and play golf. Or who seemed as if they reasonably might.

THE ADAGE "race is a country" is a cliché but nonetheless holds true. On that level the relationship between the civil rights and the hip-hop generations is akin to that between immigrants seeking opportunities and their "too Americanized" children. For us, Jim Crow is the Old Country. To the civil rights generation, the vast horizon of opportunities open to the post-civil-rights generation may well be cause for both pride and concern. The civil righters' reaction to Obama may be a barometer of their disregard for the younger hip-hop generation as well as a symptom of their own refusal to cede leadership authority. One Obama supporter who stood outside Ebenezer Baptist Church the morning he spoke there bitterly observed, "They seem to think that you don't know anything about being black unless you've been hit over the head during a voting rights march."

This was a tale partly told by the numbers. In 2008, despite the well-known indicators of ongoing struggle—poverty, incarceration, life expectancy—African Americans were clearly living in a different world than the one in which Dr. King lived and died. In that year black America was young: The median age for African Americans was 31 years, compared to 39.3 for whites. Only 8 percent of us were old enough to have direct memory of the civil rights movement, and 32 percent were too young to remember Jesse Jackson's 1988 presidential campaigns and weren't even born when he made his 1984 run. And we were more highly educated. Over 81 percent of African Americans over age 25 held a high school degree, compared to 86 percent for whites. Some 17 percent of African Americans 25 or older held bachelor's degrees; 1.1 million held advanced degrees. Over 46 percent of African American families owned the homes they lived in, and between 1990 and 2004 black Ph.D.'s doubled from 3.6 percent to 7.1 percent.

Most significantly, we were diverse. The days of the single black leader, or the elite council of leaders, tasked with moving the race forward, were gone. The needs, interests, concerns, and goals of "the black community" had so multiplied and diverged that some wondered if the term even applied. Many old presumptions could now be questioned. Young black voters—like their white counterparts—were decreasingly aligned with a single political party and more likely to register as independents. At the same time the new generation came of age against the scourge of crack and HIV in black communities; it watched history stutter as the Watts riots of 1965 were reprised in Los Angeles in 1992. Abner Louima. Amadou Diallo. Hurricane Katrina. A prison system swollen with 1.2 million black inhabitants. All were reminders that being closer was not the same thing as having arrived.[51]

Out of this context came a shared generational sensibility that was entirely aware both of racism and of opportunity, that was both black and closer to being American than W. E. B. Du Bois could have conceived when he spoke of his double consciousness and the warring halves of his soul. This generation could navigate the white world without a tour guide and had little need for the exaggerated displays of black allegiance that defined an earlier era. The louder one shouts their principles, the less one actually believes them: Following the civil rights movement, many blacks had an abiding fear of slipping into America wholesale, becoming "Afro-Saxon." But the changes wrought with the sweat and sacrifice of an earlier generation allowed those who followed to be more secure in their identities. The racial fish-out-of-water has been a staple of the American sitcom precisely because of the urge to make light of the discomfort of living in two worlds, of having dual citizenship. But the struggles of George Jefferson to thrive in America while remaining consciously, visibly, and eternally black speak less vividly to those of us who have never sipped from a colored fountain. Our identity is based upon black-and as opposed to black-or. The old questions remain in some ways; memory and history forbid them from ever disappearing completely. They just tend to be discussed at a far lower decibel.

Music, as always, provided the first theater for these generational battles. In the late 1970s and 1980s my elders commonly disregarded hip-hop as something outside the stream of black American art and tradition. Purists like jazz trumpeter Wynton Marsalis and critic Stanley Crouch took aim at the genre for lacking the sophistication and aesthetic value of their preferred art forms. In the late 1980s C. Delores Tucker, whose work with the NAACP Legal Defense Fund had helped secure voting rights for African Americans, reinvented herself as the primary nemesis of hip-hop and the social ills it most certainly midwifed. Her criticisms of its misogyny and materialism were worthy of an audience, but draped in the sanctimony of civil rights, her approach virtually assured she would not receive one. At least not from those who most needed to hear her views.

Long before Calvin Butts endorsed Hillary Clinton, he effectively defined himself for a generation through a single act. In June 1993 the reverend rented a steamroller and announced that he would use it to crush hundreds of rap CDs as a symbolic statement against "negative" music. At the last minute he aborted the plan and instead dumped the disks in front of the world headquarters of Sony music. Like Tucker's, his concern about the content of the music had an element of validity. But renting a steamroller was the definition of painting with broad strokes and brought down recriminations. The heated intergenerational exchanges that took place outside the church, two groups, invested with the same heritage, literally talked past each other.

Barack Obama was forty-five years old when he declared his candidacy for president of the United States. Like his race and his politics, his age defied simple dichotomies. Born in 1961, he grew up in a penumbra between civil rights and hip-hop, or what he would call the Moses and Joshua generations. But in age and sensibility he was close enough to the young people who flocked to his campaign to reflect their ideals, the way JFK captured the imagination of baby boomers. Nor were black young people alone: When Caroline Kennedy endorsed Obama, she noted that her children had urged her to support him. When Obama's middle name became a source of bigoted rumors about his faith and patriotism, thousands if not millions of Facebook users of all racial backgrounds inserted "Hussein" between their first and last names. But he also owed a debt to the civil rights era. The idealistic young whites adopting an Arabic middle name had grown up routinely seeing at least some images of blacks on television. They were infinitely more likely to have gone to school, played sports, or dated someone of another race than their parents. Hip-hop had been the soundtrack for their coming of age almost as much as it was to their black counterparts.

Within black America, young blacks were generally quicker

than their elders to sign on to the movement Obama was building. These were people who had not lived through the martyrdom of Martin Luther King Jr. and were that much quicker to believe fearlessly.

Anton Gunn, Obama's thirty-five-year-old South Carolina political director, virtually drafted the Democratic nominee into the hip-hop generation. "Obama is hip-hop," he said to me during the summer. "He is younger than Russell Simmons." If a generation is defined purely by age, then it includes a certain group, but if the criterion is a shared sensibility, the formative events that one witnessed, then the group is different. Regarding Obama, the generational lines are less about age than about having memories of Jim Crow and the fight for its end and being beneficiaries of that struggle. Moreover his casual swagger and personal style were deeply familiar to young people who might consider humility a character flaw.

In an interview with *Vibe* magazine Obama ticked off the names of the rappers whose music was on his iPod—Jay-Z, Ludacris—and in an interview with Jeff Johnson of BET made casual reference to rap harlequin Flavor Flav. The regard was mutual. As summer approached, Obama's name practically became an adjective in hip-hop. Common told the world in verse, "My raps ignite people like Obama." The candidate was lyrically name-checked by Jadakiss, Ice Cube, Lupe Fiasco, Lil Wayne, Juelz Santana, and Jay-Z. Nas went so far in his support as to record an entire song titled "Black President." Jay-Z performed a concert on his behalf in the crucial swing state of Michigan. In mid-April, after a bruising debate with Hillary Clinton, Obama appeared at a North Carolina rally and brushed off his shoulders—a visual quote from Jay-Z's "Dirt off Your Shoulder" that drew roars of laughter and approval. Three months later the July edition of *Vibe* ran an image of Obama brushing Bob Johnson, Hillary Clinton, Jesse Jackson, and Al Sharpton off his shoulders like so much dust.

Talib Kweli, the Brooklynite lyricist and one half of the

group Black Star, penned an open letter in support of Obama, saying in part:

> If someone asked me, I would explain why I didn't vote. It was pageantry and I wasn't with it. This was all before Barack Obama threw his hat in the ring. My criticism of the political system is that it siphons all rational thought because you have to be all things to all people. You can stand for anything doing that. I remember when Obama spoke out early against the war. I think the time he spent as a civil rights attorney on Chicago's South Side gives him a unique perspective. I often hear about his lack of experience, but his experience is one that I most closely identify with. I am not delusional about what the office of the president represents, but my support for him is just that, support for someone speaking my language.

Just after Obama clinched the nomination, Mississippi-based David Banner spoke in similar terms: "One of the things that people criticized Obama about was his lack of experience. I think that actually his power comes from the fact that he's not part of the good-old-boy network. The thing that surprised me was those older folk who didn't support him or were running against him already had their chance to change America."[52]

A musical genre premised upon a coolly cynical perspective toward political authority had no precedent for that kind of endorsement. But Will.i.am's "Yes, We Can" video had an impact upon Obama's standing with voters, particularly young ones, that was unrivaled. The simple, black-and-white montage of celebrities, backed by the words to Obama's New Hampshire concession speech, was released in early February. Within three weeks it had been viewed 26 million times and invested Barack Obama with the hopes of a generation.

The campaign understood this phenomenon intuitively. From his twenty-six-year-old speechwriter to the hundreds of college students who took a semester off to float around the country to whatever location needed volunteers, young people were its most vital reserve. Addressing the students at Howard University on September 28, 2007, Obama was at his best, bridging the gap between the responsibilities of the generations since slavery and the opportunities that lay ahead of them.

> Moses told the Joshua generation, "Don't forget where you came from." I worry sometimes that the Joshua generation in its success forgets where it came from. Thinks it doesn't have to make as many sacrifices. Thinks that the very height of ambition is to make as much money as you can, to drive the biggest car and have the biggest house and wear a Rolex watch and get your own private jet, get some of that Oprah money. And I think that's a good thing. There's nothing wrong with making money. But if you know your history, then you know that there is a certain poverty of ambition involved in simply striving just for money. Materialism alone will not fulfill the possibilities of your existence. You have to fill that with something else. You have to fill it with the golden rule. You've got to fill it with thinking about others. And if we know our history, then we will understand that that is the highest mark of service.[53]

He also gave his campaign's most serious indictment of racism. While his addresses in other black venues challenged the black community to tackle its problems, the Howard University speech was a cogent brief on the ways race still deforms American society. It was delivered by the man whose life embodied the fact that racism was no longer all-powerful.

The energy of young people fueled the campaign, but it's possible to overstate the generational divide (just as other supposed splits—the "hard-working white" divide, the Hispanic question, the class divide, the arugula gap—were actually much less

significant than hyperventilating news anchors made them out
to be). Barack Obama had a particular kinship with younger
African Americans, but he eventually found favor among blacks
of all backgrounds and ages, just as he did with 67 percent of
Hispanics and 43 percent of white voters—a larger portion than
either Bill Clinton or John Kerry received. A racial cynicism
index would show, not sharp generational breaks, but subtle
shades that got darker as age nudged upward.

In his Philadelphia speech on race, Obama talked about generational distinctions between himself and Jeremiah Wright. If
anything, he said, Wright's error was in holding a static view of
America, one shaped by the experiences of someone for whom
Jim Crow was a first-person recollection, not a memory bor-
rowed from a history book. The "race speech" left the impression that he believed racism itself was no longer an active
element in America while its "legacy" continued to have an impact. Racism was a disease that had subsided but left scars in its
wake. This conclusion was exactly what Obama's critics (and
some of his black supporters) feared most.

Even so, some younger African Americans had doubts when
it came to Obama. The tones on the racial cynicism index may
grow lighter among younger black folk, but they don't entirely
disappear. As Cornel West pointed out, older blacks who hadn't
kept track of all the wonderful changes in America weren't the
only ones who felt anger. In September in St. Petersburg three
young men disrupted an Obama speech to unfurl a banner reading WHAT ABOUT THE BLACK COMMUNITY, OBAMA?

Skepticism toward political leaders is part of American culture, and African Americans can least afford to be naïve. But this
impromptu demonstration was not about challenging leadership
as such. In a weird paradox, a black presidential candidate was
being protested by a small band of young black people—and
loudly supported by an overwhelmingly white crowd. It was one
of many inversions of history that took place all that year. This
was also the next round in the threadbare debate over Obama's
blackness.

These protesters were not part of the nostalgic fringe; they did not want Malcolm X in the White House rather than a sepia Franklin Roosevelt. During the campaign season their objection cropped up like speed bumps on the Promised Land Expressway. The rapper KRS-One lent his voice to a neurotic theory of Obama's agenda that even conspiracy theorists would have dismissed as paranoid: Any black person capable of advancing in a society with rooted hostility toward his community must have questionable ethics and allegiances. Any black person capable of reaching the White House could not possibly maintain a shred of affinity or concern for African Americans. So the thinking went.

But what *about* the black community?

In fact, the man who inspired that question began his career organizing poor people in Chicago's housing projects, to make sure they had heat and jobs. As a University of Chicago professor, Barack Obama taught a course titled "Racism and the Law," in which students read selections from Frederick Douglass, W. E. B. Du Bois, Booker T. Washington, Derrick Bell, Martin Luther King Jr., and Malcolm X; prior to 2008 a presidential candidate who had read any of those authors, much less assigned them as part of his syllabus, would have been impressive. During his time in the Illinois state senate he authored a bill intended to curb police brutality by requiring that all interrogations and confessions be videotaped. As a young lawyer, he handled pro bono employment and labor discrimination cases. In short, he had credentials worthy of the most down-for-the-cause streetcorner activist. His campaign Web site listed a series of civil rights and poverty initiatives that he supported, including job training for ex-offenders, opposition to racial profiling, and a national program to provide home nursing visits to pregnant women who cannot afford prenatal care.

Ultimately, the fears for the black community spoke to an insecurity, a fear that blacks would once again be sold a bill of goods. It had less to do with Obama himself than with his bewildering moment. For black voters, Obama's major attraction was not his civil rights platform; nor was it his pigmentation. African Americans were as weary of six years of war in Iraq and the fool's errand of remaking it, as were other ethnicities. They were as jaded by American truculence in the face of world opinion as any other citizens. More so, if the polls were to be believed. Thus Obama's support among blacks had less to do with Dr. King's dream than with George W. Bush's fantasies.

Other criticism from younger black people was less easily dismissed. Writing in the wake of Trinitygate and Obama's resignation from the church, critic Mark Anthony Neal expressed doubt about Obama's integrity. A highly placed black organizer left the campaign ahead of a crucial primary; when I spoke to her, she confessed to being frustrated by what she saw as favoritism for her white counterparts and wondered if the candidate was racially compromised. Bakari Kitwana—who authored a book titled *The Hip Hop Generation*—wondered if the campaign was giving only lip service to the needs of younger African Americans. Kitwana had spearheaded a group of activists and began raising money for the campaign.

> We raised a hundred grand and after probably twenty or thirty conversations with his camp, they wouldn't agree to a meeting with us. This was early on before he had really built up any momentum. A lot of people who work in politics felt like the campaign's response toward black people wasn't equal. I got the sense that the feeling was that black people are gonna give money anyway so let's not put ourselves in a position where we have to give something back.[54]

Meanwhile Obama was inspiring a surge of political engagement among younger black people. In Atlanta, shortly after John Lewis, 68, endorsed Clinton, activist Reverend Markel Hutchins, 30, declared that he was challenging Lewis for his congressional seat. Lewis had not faced a challenge in sixteen years. "I sincerely believe the winds of change are blowing all over this country,"

Hutchins said. And in Brooklyn, former *Vibe* magazine staff
writer Kevin Powell challenged 74-year-old Congressman Edolphus Towns, who similarly backed Clinton despite his constituents' support for Obama. Hutchins's Web site featured a
template nearly identical to that of the ObamaforAmerica site;
his campaign rented the same office space that Obama's opera-
tion had used for the Georgia primary. The Powell campaign ran
into textbook smears from the old guard: Towns cited his an-
tique activist credentials and accused the young challenger of
never having done anything in the community. Powell asked his
opponent, Wasn't the point of the civil rights movement that
younger people could have opportunities like this?

FOR ALL HIS accomplishments, Barack Obama's ultimate significance may be less as a president than as a harbinger of what
comes after his presidency. Even as he campaigned for the highest office in the land, an Obama generation was taking shape.
Neither Powell nor Hutchins was successful in his congressional
campaign. In Brooklyn, Ed Towns cruised to victory with 67 percent of the vote. John Lewis turned his campaign over to Tharon
Johnson, a thirty-one-year-old staffer who served as manager
and strategist. The effort yielded a decisive victory, as Lewis
claimed 67 percent of the vote and the remainder was divided
between Hutchins and fellow challenger Mabel Thomas. The old
operator knew what he was talking about when he told me,
"The change Obama wants is not here yet."

But it was just around the corner.

CHAPTER 6

A Tale of Two Cities

NAIROBI, DENVER, AND THE ROAD TO THE WHITE HOUSE

IF YOU DRIVE THROUGH downtown Nairobi, around the busy traffic circle on Jomo Kenyatta Avenue near the Hotel Serena where Obama stayed during his 2006 visit, you will pass a verdant slope of manicured hedges and brilliant flowers called Denver Gardens. In a city fixated on events taking place across the Atlantic, this park was one more reminder that Barack Obama's ascent marked a karmic plot twist. Denver and Nairobi are sister cities. In 1975 they cemented their relationship with an exchange of parks. City councilor (and future mayor) Nathan Kahara traveled to Colorado to oversee the opening of Nairobi Park. The Kenyans reciprocated with a green space in the center of their capital city. In the early summer of 2008, American conversations focused on delegate counts and fund-raising; but Kenyans understood the election as part of a distinct postcolonial arc. The rise of a man with immediate Kenyan ancestry into the top tiers of American power was seen as a step toward shaking off a subordinate past. The unassailable evidence was that in a few short weeks a man with roots in the Kenyan capital would make his way to the Mile High City to claim the Democratic Party's nomination for president.

The bond between Denver and Nairobi was one of several parallels and coincidences that suggested we were witnessing more than simply a brilliantly organized political campaign. Surely a divine hand was shifting the plates of history. These sentiments were not specific to Kenya. When Obama's former rival Bobby Rush announced his endorsement, he said that God had chosen Obama for the presidency (well in advance of the Electoral College seconding that choice). Spike Lee declared that an Obama victory would bring "a seismic change to the universe." It's easy to see why Obama's opponents began to parody him as a messiah.

In Nairobi people were expecting Obama not to deliver eternal salvation but to heal the blind. More specifically, they thought a man who shared their bloodlines would remedy the myopia that made the emerging world and most of Africa's concerns invisible. Time and again people told me that they expected Obama to "see" them. At the Nairobi hospital the chief neurosurgeon joked about the lingering biases of the colonial era: A white patient expresses relief that she will not be in the care of an Indian doctor, only to pass out when she learns that her surgery will actually be performed by an African. He brushed off most such incidents but recognized them as part of a broader pattern. "Most Americans don't even know that Nairobi was attacked by al Qaeda before New York was," he pointed out. The 1998 bombing of their embassy sent a shock wave through a country that had had little experience with massive, indiscriminate violence. Another Kenyan made the point to me explicitly: On some level America had been victimized on 9/11 by its own lack of vision, its inability to see that those willing to kill innocent Africans would also be willing to kill innocent Americans.

America, on the other hand, is not only visible, it's panoramic, compounding the problem and magnifying its urgency. The Kenyan hope was that Obama's perspective would benefit Africans and Americans simultaneously. Such expectations would have rested upon the shoulders of any black American contender for the presidency, not simply one with Kenyan ancestry. But Nairobi has a particular affinity for black American style and idiom. The Matatu cab drivers roll through the city in vans decorated with hip-hop motifs. A random rush hour would find weary commuters crowded into the "Jay-Z," the "Brooklyn Express," or the "Tupac/Makaveli" van circuiting the city streets. Night-clubs indistinguishable from their counterparts in Brooklyn and Miami pump dancehall and hip-hop to crowds draped in Sean John and Rocawear. Obama was now American pop culture's most compelling representative. When a government initiative to curb the consumption of dangerous home-brewed beer struck upon the idea of creating its own inexpensive brand, locals demanded that it be called Obama Beer. The initiative's leaders rejected that request but compromised by naming the brew Senator instead. One Kenyan told me that the name had significance beyond simple homage. "This is a beer created for the poor. They feel that if a son of Kenya can run for president of the United States, they can make it out of slums like Kibara."

Other streams of adulation and self-interest converged around the candidate: Vendors shouted "Obama! Obama!" to get the attention of black American tourists; a woman in the market hoped that an Obama victory would encourage blacks to spend their dollars in Kenya instead of only West Africa; a group of local business leaders began lobbying for the expansion of an airport outside Nairobi "in case Air Force One should ever need to land there."

Kenyans closely observe American politics. During the primaries people regularly gathered in hotel lobbies to watch CNN, and they debated American policy and legislation more knowledgeably than many American citizens could have. Nairobi in May 2008 proved that all politics is local. Pride swelled. But it coexisted with a widespread paranoia that Kenya would be used against Obama. Some people (including his stepmother) refused to speak about him to visitors, much less foreign media, for fear of saying something that would ruin his chances. The newspapers wondered if the Republican Party would use the socialist sympathies of Prime Minister Raila Odinga, Obama's "cousin," against him. Just months before Kenya had held its own election, followed by uncharacteristic ethnic violence, and a strand of those memories filtered into conversations about the U.S. election. Obama's family belonged to the minority Luo group, and ethnic rivalries had derailed his father's political career and propelled his life's subsequent tailspin. In Nairobi one Luo suspected that the majority Kikuyu were supporting Hillary Clinton out of concern that a President Obama would take the opportunity to pay back the insult visited upon his father. "The Luo lobby in the United States will become very powerful if he wins," she told me.

Those conversations took place across the city, the country, and even the continent, but likely nowhere as intensely as in the People's Parliament. Jeevanjee Gardens lies in Nairobi's Central District, a park dedicated to and owned by "The People." On Wednesdays people gather beneath a shaded portico to discuss Kenyan politics, history, and global affairs; following the Iowa caucuses, they discussed the prospects of Senator Barack Obama. It is a formal affair; the hundred or so participants present opening arguments, recognize a parliamentarian, set time limits, and observe formal protocols. There is no barrier to entry—it is literally the forum for the man on the street—but participants research their positions and come prepared to cite dates, statistics, and laws in support. On one particular Wednesday that spring, people raised questions about identity, race, and progress in Nairobi that were every bit as complicated as the ones surrounding Obama in America. Some believed him to be an anointed harbinger of Kenya's rising fortunes; others suspected he was a cloak to disguise a new set of colonial relationships: "He cannot do anything for Kenya—he is only there to represent the interests of the banks and financiers." An older man who also claimed to be Obama's "cousin" (the term takes on elastic definitions in the country) argued that a president who had been to Kenya would be a vast improvement over the generations of white men who had ignored the country altogether. Obama would be able to make trade initiatives that would benefit industry there; he might take an interest in Kenyan coffee growers and their desire to reach a broader market in the United States. His grandmother lives in a village in Kenya, he said; that fact has to produce some benefit for our people.

This man yielded the floor to another, who believed that such high expectations had to be tempered by reality: "The American system is divided into three portions, an executive branch, a legislative branch, and a judicial branch. He will only be in control of one of them. He cannot do anything for Kenya that the Congress doesn't approve, and they will only look out for the interests of American farmers." Between arguments, protocol could be bent, and sly jabs elicited raucous laughter.

Then a younger man emerged and changed the tenor of the discussion. "It makes no difference whether Obama's grandmother lives in Kenya or Chicago," he warned. "He cannot even understand her language." He said it with the tone of an indictment. "Obama is no Luo. He is no Kenyan. He is not even black." He was simply a brown agent of the old order, a stealth representative of the very forces that had kept Kenyans marginalized for decades. The thing he resembled most closely, he said, was a black American, and they have no interest in helping Africa either. "Where are their investments here? Why don't the rich athletes develop businesses in Africa?" A furious clash of opinions ensued. But common to all of them was the awkward attempt to come to terms with a new and thoroughly foreign reality. The young man would have been surprised by the extent to which some African Americans questioned what Obama could accomplish, even as they energetically supported his campaign.

Another set of questions emerged: What makes one African? What makes one American? Elections are not generally causes for self-reflection, but this one was, in locales as widely dispersed as Jeevanjee Gardens and Ebenezer Baptist Church. The questions were rooted deep in the history of black people on both sides of the Atlantic, but they were taken up with renewed vigor as Barack Obama—and the rest of us—inched toward November 4, 2008.

ALMOST FROM THE OUTSET Barack Obama inspired black leadership to more awkward posturing than a beginners' yoga class. On the opening night of the Democratic National Convention, a collective of black leaders furiously attempted to turn their Downward Dogs into Sun Salutations. The DNC's "Civil Rights Salute" was billed as a tribute to the leaders and activists whose sacrifices had opened the doors that Obama walked through, along with a Frankie Beverly concert, but it ended up resembling an unintentional retirement party for them. True enough, the civil rights movement was more or less minimized in discussions of Obama's ascent. But Obama laid bare the conflict of interest at the heart of the civil rights struggle. Its leaders' agenda has been to reform society in such a way as to make their own leadership unnecessary. We had not yet reached that moment, but the possibility of a black president was enough to have people worrying about their job security. And every one of those tensions was apparent at the Denver Performing Arts Center.

Maxine Waters introduced the tribute, and when Bob Johnson showed up and billionaired his way down to the front row, you could tell which way the wind was blowing. A minute later Waters was joined by Tavis Smiley. Then Danny Glover and Jackie Jackson, the wife of Jesse. By the time Al Sharpton made his way to the stage, the theme was clear. Each of them received a polite smattering of applause, but the mere mention of the words "President Obama" brought the crowd to its feet for five long minutes of whistles, cheers, and chants of "Yes we can."

We were high on the moment, this assemblage of black people who had come together to speak about Barack as our own before he gave his acceptance speech and we had to share him with the rest of the party, the country, and the world. But there's a difference between intoxication and amnesia.

The tribute recognized Johnson for "starting a business that changed the image of African Americans around the world"—which had to be the double entendre of the decade. Smiley served as emcee for part of the night and placed Barack in a roll call of black heroes stretching back to Harriet and Sojourner. Danny Glover oversaw the handing of awards to a dizzying array of national, local, semi-obscure black leaders, one of them somewhat senile. Starting with the NAACP, the plaques and praise worked their way down the list to the SCLC, whose most recent previous headline had come from its flirtation with giving Michael Vick a humanitarian award during his dog murder trial.

Undeniably those organizations all paved the way for Barack Obama's nomination, but his moment was clearly occurring over the active opposition of nearly everyone on that stage. None had forgotten Tavis's temper tantrums when Obama skipped his annual blackathon; all remembered Bob Johnson's antebellum-like allegiance to Hillary Clinton and what were widely seen as puerile attacks on Obama during the primaries. They knew that Danny Glover, humanitarian that he is, had dissed Obama in support of John Edwards. And Jackie Jackson—another Hillary supporter—was present on stage only because Jesse's castration fantasies got him uninvited from the DNC. The program seemed to be less about remembering the civil rights ancestors than about rehabilitating their contemporary counterparts. The five hundred or so people in the audience may have walked in expecting to hear "Joy and Pain," but they actually got a remix of "Redemption Song."

When Charles Steele from the SCLC strode to the podium—some two hours into the program—and began sputtering the greatest clichés of black uplift ("Know your history! Be united!") a stream of people exited the auditorium. I was among them. Outside, a drunken delegate said with the subtlety of a town crier, *That was some BULL%$#!"* Less inebriated folk pointed to the Frankie Beverly concert as a bait-and-switch, a marketing ploy for folk on the outs in the Obama era.

In the late August swelter, we did not need Steele's fulminations to know that our struggles were not over, let alone that we were living in the most exceptional, atypical, lightning-strike of moments. But it was equally clear that the first black presidential nominee had accomplished that feat over the opposition of many folk who make a living supposedly defending black interests.

Outside, Al Sharpton was seated behind a glass window, hosting a talk show about the convention. Delegates and party officials communed on sidewalks sharing admission passes for the three hundred events scheduled for that week. An ambient buzz permeated Denver in the days leading up to Barack Obama's nomination and acceptance speech. At the last minute the campaign decided to move the speech out of the Pepsi Center and into Invesco Field; hundreds of party volunteers fanned out across the city distributing tickets to ensure that they would fill the venue to capacity. Legions of security carrying assault rifles and wearing SWAT uniforms rolled through downtown in modified SUVs, while mobile billboards with pictures of aborted fetuses warned that "Obama wants to kill babies." And everywhere was the bounty.

In America glory is transformed into kitsch at an unparalleled speed. Within weeks of Iowa one could drink an Obama Soda while wearing Obama shoes and then nap in a pair of Ojamas emblazoned with the slogan YES WE CAN. That trend went into hyperdrive in Denver. Alongside John McCain condoms and George Bush toilet paper, the Obama Mall featured every imaginable consumer item that could be Obamacized. Watches bearing the candidate's face. CDs of Obama speeches backed by hip-hop beats. Obama chocolate alongside life-size Obama cutouts. And God's closet of Obama apparel: green T-shirts, black T-shirts, mauve, fuchsia, and brown T-shirts. Sober-faced Obama T-shirts, mirthful Obama, tandem-with-MLK Obama, postage stamp Obama, and Malcolm X Obama, Hope Obama, Change Obama, inscrutable Mona Lisa Obama. Eyes-toward-the-horizon Obama, union-made T-shirt Obama, James Bond Obama, radiant Obama, dressed-like-Run-DMC Obama. Obama stretched from a name into an adverb synonymous with *ubiqui-tous*. Commerce met history, high purpose with bottom line. In a word, it was America.

I arrived at this pageant as a pledged Obama delegate in the Georgia delegation. That was a story in its own right. During a canvassing trip to South Carolina, I had met a woman who later asked me to join a slate of delegates that she was organizing for Georgia's Fifth Congressional District. At the time Obama's victory was anything but certain, and a kind of partisan paranoia was taking hold among his supporters. Since delegates are not legally bound to vote for the candidate they pledge to support, many worried that Obama could win the nomination only to see it slip away at the Democratic National Convention. Others feared that the superdelegates and party establishment would close ranks around the insider candidate, Hillary Clinton. The solution, in the eyes of many, was to ensure that the Obama delegates were not party regulars or deal-making officials and were committed to voting for him. Hence the slate.

In a normal election year delegates are chosen from a pool of elected officials and connected partisans. One or two hundred people show up for a caucus to select delegates, and hopefuls are more or less assured a slot if they bring family and a few friends to vote for them. But this was not a normal year. The Obama Effect, a tide of electoral participation by people formerly outside the system, was apparent. Eighty-two people, of whom I was one, were competing for five delegate slots.

My slate bought Obama buttons in bulk and handed them out to local Democrats. To cover my expenses, I sent fund-raising e-mails to friends and set up a PayPal account. Before long I was getting second- and third-generation donations from friends of friends of friends who had received my forwarded candidacy fundraising pitch. I called in favors and got friends to form a street team for me, passing out my delegate flyers and information about the caucus. (They were about the same size and color as the party promotions people stick under your windshield at a club.)

The caucus was held on the grounds of an overheated union hall in Atlanta. Nearly fifteen hundred people crowded into the hall. Outside, the grounds resembled a political carnival. One candidate grabbed a bullhorn and climbed onto a table and began shouting his qualifications to the masses. Another had supporters handing out bottled water with his picture on the label. By lunchtime, candidates were giving away free lunches in personalized campaign paper bags. In the delegate election, we candidates each got three minutes to state our case for being elected. But because we were all competing to support the same candidate, the only way we could win was to outdo the other displays of devotion.

One person said she had traveled to three states to volunteer for Obama, which was impressive, until you heard that the next person had gone to seven. Another candidate wore a tie personally given to him by Barack himself; someone else had raised hundreds of thousands of dollars for the campaign. But the greatest-devotion-to-Obama award went to a candidate who rolled up to the microphone in a wheelchair and struggled to his feet, leaning on one of his supporters. He'd broken his leg in a car accident, he announced, while driving cross-country to volunteer for Barack. (Another contender muttered cynically that all the guy was missing was for the senator to lay hands on him so he could run around the hall shouting "I'm HEALED!") At some point in the afternoon, I looked at the crowds gathered around a table filled with free sandwiches and realized I had seriously underestimated the importance of campaign giveaways. So I took the nuclear option: I called my supporters and told them to buy every single doughnut at the local Krispy Kreme. An hour later three hundred voters high on glucose were happily reading my campaign literature. The final tally came in nearly twelve hours after the election began. Our slate had improbably won three of the five slots in the district. Afterward one man approached me and said I'd lost his vote because I'd overlooked him when handing out the Krispy Kremes. I asked if he was joking. He looked at me blankly and said, "I voted for the other guy.

He gave me a bagged lunch." I had taken all kinds of scenarios into account, but I'd never considered the possibility that I might lose an election for being soft on the pastry issue.

When I arrived in Denver as a delegate, I realized that the convention was an object lesson in political favoritism. No matter how much change Obama wanted to initiate, bedrock tiers of preference remained, sticks and carrots allocated to delegations. Delegations from reliably Democratic states were rewarded with accommodations near the convention center. Those from swing states were housed inside the downtown perimeter, still within walking distance of the daily events. But Georgia had voted Republican in 1996, 2000, and 2004, so our delegation was dispatched to a middling hotel a twenty-dollar cab ride away from all the activity. Still, ours was not the worst hand dealt by the insiders: The delegates from Michigan and Florida, the centers of so much dispute and anxiety during the primaries, were exiled to a motel outside the city limits.

On the opening Monday morning we delegates awoke to a screaming declaration in *USA Today*: HILLARY SUPPORTERS RESTLESS. Only 47 percent of Clinton supporters would be willing to support Obama, the article said. That story confirmed our worst suspicions. Truth told, I'd seen low-intensity skirmishes between the two camps since the night I arrived in Denver. The smallest slight—a declined dinner invitation, a missed meeting—became part of the matrix of suspicion. Paranoid rumors floated that Clinton Democrats were holding secret meetings and plotting to derail the convention.

Some of the rumors were well founded. Clinton delegates openly spoke of derailing Obama's nomination and initiating a disastrous floor fight. A week before the convention I received an e-mail urging me to abandon Obama and support Clinton in Denver. I sent a simple two-word reply. (It wasn't "No thanks.") The media streamed stories about PUMAs (Party Unity My Ass), disgruntled Clinton Democrats planning to make Denver into a remake of the disastrous 1968 convention. Others were less apocalyptic but no more reassuring. When I asked one Clinton delegate if he would be willing to support Obama, he said, "Let's see what happens on Wednesday"—the night Clinton's name would be placed in nomination.

Inside the Pepsi Center the stagecraft was elaborate. I wondered if Obama's youth, energy, and fluency in pop culture influenced the music chosen for the convention. Between speeches Democratic deejays offered servings of Earth, Wind & Fire's "Dancing in September," though technically it was late August; Lenny Kravitz's "Are You Gonna Go My Way?"—the question directed at Clinton's supporters; James Brown's "Funky Good Time," which inspired ten thousand people to sing, "We gonna take it hiiiiigher!" I hoped they would follow it with "Funky President." Then came Kool & the Gang's "Celebration," for obvious reasons; Carlos Santana's "Oye Como Va"; and Stevie Wonder's "Isn't She Lovely," played as Michelle Obama was leaving the stage, for even more obvious reasons. The choice of music seemed too deliberate, in fact, when Bill Clinton's Wednesday-night address was followed by Robert Palmer's "Addicted to Love." Not all the lingering animus came from the Clinton camp.

On the opening night Michelle Obama gave the keynote. Some observers had wondered if the country was more resistant to the idea of a black president or a black first lady. Weeks earlier the *New Yorker* ran a flat satire of Michelle Obama and her husband, he cloaked in Islamic garb, she dressed like a new Angela Davis, the two sharing what Fox News slurred as a "terrorist fist jab." The inept humor reflected the fact that the image was too close to how people actually perceived the two. In the Atlanta airport I saw a man drag his wife over to the newsstand to show her the image. The attempted comedy was lost on him; he told her the nation was perilously close to electing an al-Qaeda sympathizer as president. Such incidents, magnified and multiplied over twenty-two months of campaigning, refracted and contorted through the lens of cable news, and blasted through the blogosphere made a distorted image of the Obamas seem perilously realistic to many.

Those who witnessed it, even for after seconds, immediately recognized the meaning of Obama Green. Michelle invented that shade in the twenty feet that separated the entrance to the Democratic National Convention from the podium. To say that she was elegant in her green dress was like saying that summer is hot or butter is smooth—the cliché was so apt, so consistent, that it warranted repetition.

Wearing Obama Green was hardly the greatest of her accomplishments, but it couldn't be dismissed either, because even before her flawless elocution brought grown men to tears, this gifted and graceful-tall black woman sidestepped the simpleton categories handed down for her. Her mere presence on that stage forced all of us to expand our vocabulary.

The ancient language of race and gender in this country offers no adequate words for Michelle, or women like her. So it's no surprise that assorted hacks and haters in the media fell back on their mother tongue, calling her "baby-mama," "angry black woman."

Nor, alas, did black folk hold the upper hand here. We knew that Michelle existed before the rest of the world did, but we'd buried the appropriate words for her in an unmarked grave and covered it with assorted b-words, h-words, and every lame offering ever shouted with a gold-tooth glint from the passenger side of a car. So as she was walking those twenty feet, Michelle was not so much stepping up to a podium as stepping outside of a box. Meanwhile organizers passed out placards with MICHELLE printed on them, for us to pass down to our fellow delegates. Many refused to play nice, and normally staid delegates strong-armed them. After the convention closed for the night, the hall was littered with CHANGE WE CAN BELIEVE IN and COMMON VALUES, COMMON GOALS signs, but not one of those bearing Michelle's name was left behind. One man waded through the crowd, holding his MICHELLE sign high above his head, and said, "I'm bringing this back home for my girls."

Michelle Obama may yet exist as a muse for toxic commentators, but if the nation were capable of honestly comparing her with Cindy McCain, we knew what would happen. Only in the dark arcs of the American media would a black woman from the South Side of Chicago have to prove that she's a "regular" woman, while a woman who inherited $100 million is assumed to be just like everyone else.

And then she said:

> The American dream is a blessing hard won by those who came before me, all of them driven by the same conviction that drove my dad to get up an hour early each day to painstakingly dress himself for work, the same conviction that drives the men and women I've met all across this country. People who work the day shift, they kiss their kids goodnight, and head out for the night shift, without disappointment, without regret, see, that goodnight kiss is a reminder of everything they're working for.

And she offered a testament to her husband:

> He's the same man who drove me and our new baby daughter home from the hospital ten years ago this summer, inching along at a snail's pace, peering at us anxiously at—through the rearview mirror, feeling the whole weight of her future in his hands, determined to give her everything he'd struggled so hard for himself, determined to give her something he never had, the affirming embrace of a father's love.

She concluded with a declaration:

> And as I tuck that little girl . . . and her little sister into bed at night, you see, I think about how, one day, they'll have families of their own and how, one day, they—and

your sons and daughters—will tell their own children
about what we did together in this election.

They'll tell them how this time we listened to our
hopes, instead of our fears . . . how this time we decided to stop doubting and to start dreaming . . . how
this time, in this great country, where a girl from the
South Side of Chicago can go to college and law school,
and the son of a single mother from Hawaii can go all
the way to the White House . . . how this time we committed ourselves to building the world as it should be.

During almost every other speech the normal buzz of business being done continued, but none of that with her. When she
finished, the delegate next to me just shook his head, wondering
how he'd foolishly believed there was only one orator in the
Obama family.

As I listened to that speech, it was impossible for me not to
hear echoes of Fannie Lou Hamer and her interracial band of
democratic dreamers. She'd come to the 1964 Atlantic City Democratic National Convention, attempting to end segregation in
politics at a time when the words *integrated* and *Mississippi* could
not fit within the same sentence.

When the Mississippi Freedom Democratic Party was denied
seating at the convention, Hamer famously asked, "Is this
America?" An alumna of a Mississippi cotton field, she knew
eviction and lack; she understood America in the way that the
janitors understood the Empire State Building, from deep inside
the steam vents and far, far below the surface. But here is the
jewel: Even knowing all that, Hamer still offered the question:
"Is this America?" The fact that it was still an open question
meant that she had granted that cold-shouldering nation the
benefit of the doubt; she had accepted the possibilty that a
country could be bigger than a cotton field. Hamer, as much
as anyone, authored the circumstances in which an Obama—
Barack or Michelle—could step into prominence.

Michelle Obama came from far different circumstances. A Harvard lawyer has a different arrangement from a sharecropper. But still they shared a song that most of us knew by heart. Hamer's people later deserted Mississippi for Chicago by the trainload, and likely some person who worked the fields with Hamer later walked down Michelle Obama's street on the South Side.

A road led directly from Atlantic City to Denver, and on August 25, 2008, Michelle Obama etched its road map. The charge from her speech accompanied the delegates as they poured out of the building and into the Denver night.

Jimmy Carter addressed the Georgia delegation the following morning. He had long before grown comfortable in his role as elder statesman, and despite some lingering acrimony from his recent book on the Israeli-Palestinian situation, he remained one of the more highly regarded Democrats in the party. For that reason alone, many had expected he would address the convention, if only briefly. But Carter was not allowed to speak. He should have been. As he told the delegation, he was "the world's foremost authority on divided conventions." In 1976, when fractures in the Republican Party split the Ford supporters from the Reagan bloc, Carter had been the beneficiary. But four years later the divisions between Carter and Kennedy Democrats helped sink his reelection bid. John McCain had no movement backing him as Ronald Reagan did, but Carter's point was clear to everyone in the room.

The tension in the hall peaked when Hillary Clinton strode to the podium that night. Fifteen minutes into her speech she said, "No way, no how, no McCain," and even the Obama delegates leaped to their feet waving HILLARY signs. To say it was a great speech would be to damn it with understatement. Ironically, the best-delivered speech of her campaign was her endorsement of her chief rival. If offered catchy metaphors ("We are on the same team and none of us can sit on the sidelines"), sharp rhetorical questions ("I want you to ask yourself, were you in this campaign just for me or for that young marine and others like him?"), and deft recastings of history:

> My mother was born before women could vote. But in this election my daughter got to vote for her mother for President. This is the story of America. Of women and men who defy the odds and never give up. How do we give this country back to them? By following the example of a brave New Yorker, a woman who risked her life to shepherd slaves along the Underground Railroad.
>
> And on that path to freedom, Harriet Tubman had one piece of advice. If you hear the dogs, keep going. If you see the torches in the woods, keep going. If they're shouting after you, keep going. Don't ever stop. Keep going. If you want a taste of freedom, keep going. Even in the darkest of moments, ordinary Americans have found the faith to keep going.

The history professor side of me had to give it up when she brought Harriet Tubman into the equation. The realist in me recognized that the Harriet Tubman reference was calibrated to soothe those angry black Democrats in New York whom she would need if she wanted to retain her Senate seat. The media quibbled and diagrammed sentences trying to decipher a hidden insult to Barack. But by honest standards that was one of the strongest endorsement speeches in the party's history.

Outside, a knot of her supporters still voiced their doubts about Obama. One reiterated exhausted claims that the DNC rules—although written by Clinton's own adviser—were unfair and favored the undeserving Obama. They were what Donald Rumsfeld once called the bitter-enders. But the storyline was already changing. For weeks beforehand the media had covered the exploits of the PUMAs, but on the night of the formal nomination they numbered fewer than a dozen, including the children there with their parents. The real question was whether a groundswell of Clinton supporters would simply drop out of the process. Among the Obama delegates, the response was akin to what the delegate had told me on the first night: "Great words, but we'll see what happens in November."

JUST OUTSIDE THE PEPSI CENTER in Denver is a strip of landscaped greenery, encased by a three-foot-high white granite wall. A Kenyan proverb is engraved into the wall: "We do not inherit the earth from our parents, we borrow it from our children." On nomination night the path was accessorized by two white men holding a huge banner bearing the words "Rednecks for Obama." It was a study in contrasts.

The scripted drama of the nomination (and the fact that no one knew it was scripted drama at the time) intensified the moment. First delegations distributed formal ballots and placed their candidate's name into nomination. Then came the alphabetical arrangement of states and the formal delegate count. Curiously large delegations abstained, sending a murmur of concern through the gathering. Next the flea-flicker arrangement of nominations, tossed to Illinois, who then pitched it back to New York, allowing Hillary Clinton to call for an acclimation vote. Observers later noted that virtually no time lapsed between the moment when Nancy Pelosi said, "All opposed say nay" and the one when her gavel landed and she declared, "The ayes have it."

That stunning bit of choreography highlighted something that Clinton's most die-hard supporters had missed: Their hopes of a nomination fight harked back to an era when conventions actually had something to do with selecting candidates. At this point they are closer to Broadway productions, with everyone memorizing their lines and dancing on cue. Each sign is carefully printed, distributed, and coordinated with the speech where it will be waved. The cameras are angled and ready to catch a shot of the delegate with tear-stained cheeks and an American-flag top hat. Heated arguments still occur in smoke-filled rooms—they just do so in May and June, long before the delegates have begun packing.

Still, at least one portion of the event was unstaged. In the moments following the vote, people left the convention hall in a mass exodus. The convention had not adjourned for the evening; they simply walked out, needing to be outside, to discuss what they had just done, to finger the texture of history. Joseph Lowery sat in a wheelchair in the hall, surrounded by a chattering crowd of admirers posing for pictures, asking his thoughts, thanking him for his early support for Barack Obama. The eighty-year-old retired pastor gracefully endured his groupies. He thought of the moment as a revival: "I thank God I lived long enough to see this day." At other times he confessed to wondering if God had kept him alive, past the deaths of his colleagues and brothers from the civil rights days, in order for him to support the young candidate. Ray Nagin, mayor of New Orleans, admitted to a delegate, "This was something I never thought I would see in my lifetime." Bob Johnson told a younger man that he was committed to following Hillary Clinton's lead in supporting the nominee, and then he said, "This moment is equal to the most significant moment in African American history, the Emancipation Proclamation in 1863." Maxine Waters praised it as one of the most historic moments of her life. A congressional staffer told me that as the votes were being tallied, he stood backstage, the only black man in the room, and when the final acclimation vote was reached, he wept openly.

That scene replayed itself across the convention hall and out into the city and country and world. Kenyans stayed up all night for news of the nomination, which came at five A.M. in Nairobi. Newspapers ran blaring headlines of Obama's accomplishment, and people scoured the city for campaign buttons and stickers, which had been scarce to that point. In the nearly eight months since Obama's stunning Iowa upset, the candidates had slogged through town halls, debates, rallies, interviews, strategy sessions, fund-raising drives, small victories, and grand setbacks. The yield was a presidential nominee, the first African American to hold that title, but also one for whom focusing on a racial adjective seemed to diminish so much else that was unprecedented.

Somehow referring to him as the "first black" managed to en-capsulate centuries of history and still miss the point.

Barack Obama accepted the Democratic nomination for the presidency on August 28, 2008, the forty-fifth anniversary of Dr. King's "I Have A Dream" speech, delivered during the March on Washington. It is also the anniversary of the day in 1955 when Emmett Till was brutally beaten and his lifeless body sub-merged in the muddy Tallahatchie River. Congressman John Lewis, the sole surviving speaker from the March on Washing-ton, had come full circle from the weeks when angry constituents bombarded his office with demands that he support Barack Obama. It was fitting that he should be the one to open the pro-ceedings that evening.

On the night of the acceptance speech, Mile High Stadium was like a fortress. Federal officers with assault rifles were posi-tioned atop the walls and at every entrance. Denver's municipal police force was swollen by ranks of law enforcement who had driven in from around the country. The suspicion had a demo-cratic quality: On the way in I saw a billionaire and her personal bodyguards being frisked. Actors and celebrities stood in line with the people who watched them on television, all awaiting a security clearance. On the flight back to Atlanta I sat next to a Treasury agent who told me that fifteen hundred officers had been assigned to guard the building alone and treat it as if it were a person. His commanding officer had sent them out with the admonition, "If anything happens to that man, you have all just resigned from the Secret Service." That solemn charge was reiterated after word of arrests in a suspected assassination plot made its way around the convention.

Here are the memories I brought home from Denver: Literal miles of people lined up to get into Invesco Field. Rows of phone banks at the front of the stadium, where people could sit down and call voters and encourage them to support the candi-date. The crowd of eighty thousand people doing the wave be-fore John Lewis came out to give his speech. The fact that I sat directly in front of the podium, ten rows back, close enough to take pics of the first black presidential nominee, without having to hit the zoom button on my camera. The ripple that went through the crowd when Barack nearly shouted "Enough!" to John McCain's distortions, and the man next to me who said, "He's about to take this back to the South Side."

But overall the speech was most remarkable for its restraint. For months Obama had been parodied, first by Clinton and then by McCain, as a vacuous pretty girl. But this speech, unlike the one he gave in New Hampshire, was much more about mechanics than poetry. In a measure of his campaign's discipline, he resisted the temptation to turn Mile High Stadium into a down-home revival. Another "Yes We Can" moment, and Obama would have written the GOP talking points for them: "See, we told you he's just a motivational speaker." Instead he spoke about details and policies, playing the dozens with John McCain: "He says he'll follow Bin Laden to the gates of hell; he won't even follow him to the cave where he lives." In an odd way, the speech was inspiring for its lack of inspiration.

Days earlier I'd talked to an activist who pointed out that the GOP had won seven of the preceding ten presidential elections largely because of its success in creating a big tent. The Republicans had managed, however improbably, to get an unemployed factory worker to vote for the same candidate as the millionaire CEO who just fired him. But progressives, she said, had the opposite of a tent—they had a funnel. They took the broadest possibilities and narrowed them down to a handful of ideologically correct, but absolutely unelectable figures, thereby choosing defeat over the kinds of compromise implicit within democracy. By that means powerlessness becomes a consolation prize that allows ideals to remain unblemished.

I thought about that conversation again after I heard Cornel West and Julianne Malveaux savage Barack Obama's acceptance speech on Tavis Smiley's talk show that night. Malveaux went hypertensive because Barack never mentioned Dr. King by name (despite the fact that he had had two of Dr. King's children and Congressman John Lewis speak about the March on Washington and that only the absolute dimmest of bulbs could not know who that "young preacher from Georgia" he mentioned was). West fulminated that Obama had left out a "critique of white supremacy" and missed the symbolism of the moment. And worst of all, he noted, "no one was crying."

Obama had been giving inspirational speeches for months. He'd built a grassroots machine and brought people into active political engagement who had sworn off politics long ago. But conventions are about winning elections, plain and simple. Most of those gathered in Mile High that night hoped Obama would avoid the kind of emotive speech he was famous for and deliver exactly what he did: a basic outline of his policy positions. The measure of Obama's connection to those movements West was talking about was not whether he mentioned them in his acceptance speech but whether he prioritized them in the White House—and that meant he had to first win the election.

Inside Invesco Field the acceptance speech inspired a clear-eyed euphoria. During key points the Obama delegates shared nods and hand-slaps. A friend who had always been deeply skeptical of the rituals of patriotism sent out a mass e-mail with the subject line "Last Night I Waved an American Flag." In a curious bit of synchronicity, the PBS camera caught me waving a flag, and I got several texts from friends at home who saw me on television. I am not a waver of flags. In high school a teacher once chastised me for revising the last line of the Pledge of Allegiance to say "with liberty and justice for whites."

Obama's nomination didn't change history, it didn't eliminate the reasons why I substituted *whites* for *all* in ninth-grade assembly; it didn't remove my discomfort with true-believer patriotism for which flag-waving and pledge-reciting is an actual measure of devotion to citizenship. But it did remind me of the tradition of people who sought to revise the meaning of those symbols. It reminded me that the same flag that oversaw and protected chattel slavery was also carried by men and women who sought to abolish it.

Obama seemed to have grown over the course of the campaign. He'd begun as an intriguing upstart, but ever since his trip to Israel in July, I'd had the impression that he actually looked presidential. In Denver he looked every bit the statesman, capable of carrying the weight that comes with that presidential seal. Not that the transformation came without its costs. At one point he turned his head to the left, and on the massive screen just to the right of the stage, you could see how much gray hair he had amassed. People seeing him for the first time would not have referred to him as a "youthful candidate"—or at least not as often as they did twenty months earlier.

Obama accepted the nomination, and had you turned your head at the right moment, you would've caught sight of a screen showing Dr. King and snipers positioned on top of that screen. He finished his speech, and the confetti cannon went off just a moment too soon. Our whole row of delegates jumped at the sound; no one needed to ask why. This was progress, even if we were still waiting for the other shoe to drop.

On the way out of the stadium, the delegation was already plotting voter-registration strategies and making get-out-the-vote plans. The flag-waving and pledge-reciting were behind us. The acceptance speech marked the formal end of the epic primary campaign. The Republican Party was less than eight hours away from announcing Sarah Palin as its vice-presidential pick. The real work was just getting started.

CHAPTER 7

Mandates and Metaphors

OF LINCOLN, ROOSEVELT, AND OBAMA

BEFORE BARACK OBAMA could change America, America had had to change. On the first Tuesday in November, millions around the world gathered to watch the election results. The iconic moment, the one destined for headlines, blog pages, textbooks, and permanent memory came when a new president stood before a vast assemblage in Grant Park in Chicago and said, "Change has come to America." But the man uttering those words was as much a beneficiary of change as an agent of it. The integration of schools, voting rights protections, and employment discrimination laws had all been treatments, not cures, for the affliction of racism. For decades we had wondered whether we were simply treating symptoms while the actual disease continued to metastasize. The devastation of Hurricane Katrina revealed a racial line, another indicator of relapse. The drowning city, the bloated black bodies drifting down the avenues, the private militias and neighboring towns that armed themselves fearing an incursion of lawless blacks, the rapper Kanye West declaring on air that the president "doesn't care about black people"—these images from that tempest in no way resemble a society that was just three years away from electing an African-American president.

In focusing on the major events, we missed a more important subplot. Invisible, incremental changes accrue beneath the surface until we reach a threshold, and suddenly the world is massively different. It's the type of thing we expect to notice, but it is amazing how often we don't. The Soviet Union appeared impregnable to its outside observers—until it simply crumbled into history. Billions of dollars had been spent for espionage, analysis, and strategy, yet the United States was as stunned as the rest of the world when the country against which it defined itself collapsed under its own weight. Apartheid looked to be as permanent as the Capetown Mountains—until it fell to pieces, and a nation defined by racial segregation elected its chief dissident to the presidency.

Much like the clueless analysts at Langley on the verge of the Soviet demise, observers of American society failed to see the groundswell of change that preceded Barack Obama's candidacy, let alone his election. A few weeks after the election, at a conference about the historic event we had just witnessed, I asked a panel of political scientists, historians, and sociologists, "What did we miss?" In response I received a moment of silence and a few skeletal theories. The fact is that the 2008 election was what Donald Rumsfeld once referred to as an "unknown unknown." And sometimes even hindsight gives you only a partial view.

Once the campaign gained momentum, tracking changes had become a cottage industry. Established Web sites like the Gallup Poll's saw an increase in traffic. Nate Silver's excellent Fivethirty eight.com and other sites sprang up to feed the limitless public appetite for new data and hints as to what it all meant. The media incorporated a wider array of voices in the hope of gaining a perspective they'd previously missed. (Turning on cable news during one particularly heated stretch of the campaign, I nearly mistook CNN for BET.) But the truth was that black people were just as, if not more, shocked than everyone else.

Election day came scarcely nine weeks after the conventions

ended. Aside from a temporary blip in the opposition's poll numbers following the selection of Sarah Palin, Obama drew a commanding lead over McCain, driven, inscrutably, by the lagging economy. Cable news hysteria nonetheless continued, and fractional insights of polls moved to smaller and smaller subsets, verging on the realization that America is a nation of 290 million individual demographic trends. Thus for every scraplet of data, an anecdote was waiting to affirm it if you dug deep enough. Obama couldn't "close the deal" (whatever that meant). Hispanics would vote for McCain because they couldn't stand the thought of blacks moving ahead of them politically. Sarah Palin the celebrity would neutralize Obama the celebrity, leaving John McCain to pick up votes and eventually the White House. The only poll data that ultimately mattered was the final one, which read, Barack Obama 365, John McCain 173.

Race was not the only thing that changed that evening, although we discussed it first. We discussed how McCain's choice of Palin had not only sunk his candidacy but represented the demise of an entire genre of politics. The Republican Party once dreamed of having a populist movement to combat the grassroots fervor of the 1960s Left, but the arranged marriage between himself and the Alaska governor made it clear that the era of the libertarian Goldwater Republican was gone, done in by pandering to plumbers and torch-bearing villagers at the rallies. Commentators bandied the word *terrorism* but made only scant references to Jeremiah Wright. The relentless dissection of Wright during the spring had effectively immunized the campaign from that issue during the fall—one of the numerous debts Obama owed Hillary Clinton.

Barack Obama did not squeak into office. He eclipsed his Republican rival by eight million votes; his 365 electoral votes were more than double those of John McCain. Obama won 53 percent of the popular vote, a higher portion than George W. Bush in either 2000 or 2004, Bill Clinton in 1992 or 1996, and equal to that of George H. W. Bush in 1988. His tally was higher than that of any Democratic president since Lyndon B. Johnson won 61 percent in 1964. He arrived with a mandate written by history and delivered by the voters themselves.

The obvious racial barrier was broken, but the nature of his mandate was as consequential as the melanin content of his skin. The 192-vote margin in the Electoral College marked a decisive rejection of John McCain and, more viscerally, the preceding eight years of George W. Bush. But it wasn't an electoral blowout. Reagan had crushed Jimmy Carter 489 to 49 in 1980; Nixon steamrolled McGovern 520 to 17 in 1972; and Johnson had embarrassed Goldwater 486 to 52. Obama couldn't lay claim to the 512-point spread that separated Reagan and Mondale in 1984, yet his position was, in some ways, unique.

Barack Obama arrived in Chicago as a young idealistic college graduate in 1983. His political education came from two sources: the community organizing tradition of Saul Alinsky, and the Daley machine politics that preceded and followed the 1983–87 tenure of Mayor Harold Washington. Alinsky had been deeply skeptical of politicians and believed that all coalitions should be both temporary and governed by self-interest. Early in his career a group of community activists swooned over the Chicago mayor after their efforts forced him to visit their neighborhood. The sight disturbed him, because they believed that the power for change lay in the mayor's hands, not their own. Politicians, in his view, were to be bargained with, not fawned over. That early insight would come through again and again in the rhetoric of the campaign. His speeches were spiced with phrases like "I can't do it alone" and "We can bring about change," conveying the sense that the rallies were a conversation among equals, even if only one of them had Secret Service protection. Paradoxically, Obama's campaign was based upon grassroots empowerment but was most often criticized—sometimes rightly—as a cult of personality. In that way he had more in common with Dr. King than we would commonly observe. Comparisons with King became the cliché of 2008, literally the stuff of T-shirts and dorm room art. But few besides Dr. King would have understood the paradox at the heart of the campaign and remembered that presidents are to be held accountable, not gushed over.

Chicago was a crucial part of Obama's political education. The regimes of the first and second Daley leveraged favoritism, nepotism, and good grace as political currency, as all machines do. While Alinsky's community organizing sought to diminish the needs of the individual in favor of the many, the machine seeks to do just the opposite. Every pothill filled, every park cleaned, every crime solved is a gift demonstrating the good graces of the boss. In a dictatorship (the highest expression of a machine) the tyrant's face is always plastered on billboards, school textbooks, and currency. Since the days of Boss Tweed and Huey Long political machines have been driven by charismatic men of outsize charm and outsize appetites. Where the community organizer seeks to diffuse power throughout society, the machine seeks to concentrate it in the hands of a very few.

Amazingly, Obama's campaign bore the fingerprints of both: It was an effort located somewhere between Alinksy and Daley. Charisma was the oil, and fuel came from the grassroots. Where a machine gathers funding from a handful of fat cats, a movement seeks to raise millions of small offerings. Where a machine uses smoke-filled back rooms and accesses those who populate them, a movement draws its strength from outside the corridors of power. At varying times both traits defined Obama's campaign. It out-fund-raised the Clinton campaign using the technology of social networking sites to garner hundreds of thousands of small donations. At the same time it won the endorsement of powerful Democratic Party figures like Ted Kennedy—something that other "movement candidates" of recent years could not have hoped to do.

After election day it translated into a mandate: a database with twelve million supporters' names organized by state, congressional district, and zip code, many of them eager to continue their involvement. The fund-raising list included 1.5 million individual donors. And the new administration had a capacity to treat the White House as if it were itself a grassroots movement. Where previous executives arm-twisted for concessions from the legislative branch, this one had an unrivaled capacity to agitate voters in a given congressman's home district or to dial up local pressure to offset lobbyists. For decades the term *judicial activism* has been a term of derision; Obama's election inaugurated the possibility of *presidential activism*.

In 1999 software engineer Linus Torvalds offered the world a radical proposition: "open source" software, programs that are free and created by an unnumbered mass of collaborators. Obama offers the opportunity for the first "open source" presidency. The 1.5 million in is fund-raising network were literally invested in his brand identity. Barackobama.com was specifically built in keeping with the social networking software behind Facebook's success. The message boards on the site quickly became a rolling debate forum, in which supporters critiqued and dissented (sometimes vigorously) from their candidate's opinions. That openness represented a contrast from the previous administration, which had bristled at criticism, operated on a payback ethic, and antagonized its critics.

The openness, however, had pitfalls. Most presidents are deeply indebted to a handful of people; Obama's White House is broadly indebted to millions of people. That created, almost from the outset, an immense potential for disappointment. A tent can be only so big before the roof begins to sag. Even during the summer of 2008 the media reported disappointment from Ralph Nader ("He's acting white"), Mu'ammar Gadhafi ("He's a lackey of Israel"), various outposts of the black left ("He attacked the black community for father's day"), the netroots ("How could he support the FISA [Foreign Intelligence Surveillance Act] bill?"), and the Muslim community ("He's keeping us at arm's length")—all in the same week.

An ancient principle of politics, quickly revealed to all new regimes, is that winning power is easier than administering it. Campaigning, even in the brutal crucible of 2008, is simpler than governing. And amid war and economic crises, governing is a magnitude more difficult. Still, those concerns were less than background noise in Grant Park. That day and those immediately following saw all manner of counterintuitive moments: Dick Cheney offered an awkward reminiscence of his arrival in a still-segregated Washington, years earlier; and John McCain gave a concession speech more eloquent than anything he'd said on the campaign trail. The president-elect wandered around the South Side of Chicago with a Secret Service detail. Change had come to America. And all of America was trying to figure out exactly what that meant.

THE LONG CAMPAIGN had conjured one set of metaphors; the election brought another hastily assigned group of them. It was only natural for people to break a foreign experience down into smaller analogies. From one quarter, Obama's election brought forth mentions of Emancipation and Reconstruction; in other spheres, the conversation turned to FDR and Lincoln. No one mentioned the Apollo landing, but it would not have been exceptional if they had. The nation seemed united, if not by the election, then by the need to understand what the election meant. But no previous event, no single happening, offered a one-to-one correspondence. This was a unique juncture in our history. Still, a few granules of meaning could be found in the comparisons.

Among the many plot twists in the 2008 campaign was the return of Franklin Roosevelt as a political icon. After suffering years of disparagement as the architect of big government, the deepening economic crisis gave many Americans a new appreciation for the thirty-second president. Advisers to President-elect Obama reportedly read up on New Deal policy as they prepared to take office, and *Time* magazine featured Obama on the cover in a remake of the famous top-hat-and-cigarette-holder image of FDR.

One reason for the comparison between Obama and Roosevelt was the trying economic and military circumstances that

Obama inherited. Moreover both men owed their election in part to unpopular Republican administrations accused of mishandling and underregulating the market. And both elections marked a turning point in the political history of African Americans. FDR's New Deal successfully attracted African Americans who had been loyal to "the party of Lincoln" for over half a century; Obama's election as president strengthened the fraying bonds between African Americans and Democrats.

Both of their Republican predecessors were tied to the mishandling of a national catastrophe: The Bush administration's ineptitude in Hurricane Katrina's aftermath was the biggest disaster-relief failure in decades; Herbert Hoover, as secretary of commerce, had overseen the Mississippi flood of 1927, where black sharecroppers were rounded up and forced at gunpoint to repair breached levees. Both Roosevelt and Obama faced strident Republican criticism: Roosevelt's chief critics were a Louisiana governor (Huey Long) and a right-wing radio host (Father Coughlin), whereas Obama had scarcely received the election results before observers began weighing in on Louisiana governor Bobby Jindal's prospects and Rush Limbaugh told the world he hoped the new president would fail.

But the most telling connection between Roosevelt and Obama was one that was most commonly overlooked: their membership in groups that have historically suffered from discrimination. Roosevelt was stricken with polio at age thirty-nine and eventually was confined to a wheelchair; he and Obama, the first African-American president, were tied together on the level of symbolism.

At least since his victory in the Iowa caucuses, Barack Obama had been viewed as a harbinger of the postracial society. Shortly after he won the general election, the *Wall Street Journal* said that his victory would end "the myth of racism as a barrier to achievement." Indeed, the willingness of millions of white Americans to vote for a black presidential candidate made it hard to imagine a circumstance in which race still mattered. And

Roosevelt's experience—as the first disabled president—actually became pertinent to the Obama discussion.

Disability and blackness were understood in surprisingly similar ways in American history; both were purported by the mainstream to be physical markers of difference and inferiority. In the nineteenth century skin color was intricately connected to biases and superstitions about disability. Republican Thaddeus Stevens, for instance, attributed his lifelong support of black causes to his deformed foot: It provided him insight into what it felt like to be ostracized on the basis of an arbitrary physical characteristic. During the rise of Jim Crow, hopeful immigrants at Ellis Island were being screened to weed out those with disabilities and birth defects.

Given that history, the ascent of a wheelchair-bound president would seem to mark a leap forward for disabled Americans. It was and it wasn't. The complexities of Roosevelt's situation provide insight into the social landscape in the wake of Barack Obama's election. In fact, Roosevelt's experience seems to point to a kind of uneven progress where we move forward as a society but not uniformly. In terms of getting beyond bigotry, the presidency may actually be ahead of the rest of American society.

In the way that Roosevelt had to manage his disability—many Americans weren't aware of it at the time; in a kind of symmetry, Obama carefully managed race as a topic during the campaign. The fact that disabled people and African Americans could be represented in the White House marked an undeniable breakthrough, but neither Roosevelt nor Obama could afford to dwell on that fact in their campaigns. Thus aspects of their identity that spoke most clearly to their character and fortitude were, in some ways, political liabilities. That irony was present in 1997, when the Roosevelt memorial was built on the National Mall. The image obscures not only Roosevelt's wheelchair but also the inspiring fact that the man who led the United States through its worst economic trial and its greatest military triumph did so despite a physical disability. The National Parks Service's decision to literally cloak his disability generated so much criticism from advocates of disabled rights that a second sculpture of him in a wheelchair was constructed.

Barack Obama's election didn't automatically elevate the nation beyond race, any more than Roosevelt's automatically erased bias against the disabled. In 2007 the Equal Employment Opportunity Commission received 30,510 racial discrimination complaints that resulted in $67.7 million in monetary benefits for plaintiffs, not including monies awarded through litigation. Amid the euphoria over the election, it seemed almost distasteful to bring up the nagging racial disparities in health care, in life expectancy, in income, and in the criminal justice system, none of which seemed poised to disappear on inauguration day.[55]

THE MOST PROMINENT presidential comparison, between Obama and Lincoln, was both more understandable and more vexing. Pondering the bond between the Great Emancipator and the Brother-in-Chief placed a handle on a moment that was otherwise difficult to grasp. The 2008 election could then be neatly catalogued as a bookend to Lincoln's election and the war over the meaning of race and freedom. A long line of figures, both contemporary and historical, have seen something of Lincoln in themselves and have had no objection to sharing that observation with others. None of them shared the surface similarities that Obama could claim, coincidences that, given his racial background and Lincoln's connection to Emancipation, made the comparison seem all the more apt. Both were tall, lanky lawyers who had migrated to Illinois from elsewhere, served in the state legislature, and been involved in Senate races that inadvertently became microcosms of broader national concerns. When Abraham Lincoln met Stephen Douglas for seven debates ahead of their 1856 contest for the Senate, the issue of slavery was at the forefront of national consciousness; Obama's Senate race pitted him against a succession of unwieldy Republicans, and his opposition to the war in Iraq ensured that the election would take on even broader significance. Obama took office just a month ahead of the bicentennial of Lincoln's birth and chose "A New Birth of Freedom," a phrase taken from the Gettysburg Address, as the inaugural theme.

Obama played up that angle, choosing to announce his campaign for the White House on the steps of the old capitol that Lincoln's efforts helped build and where he delivered his famed "House Divided" speech. Two years later Obama mirrored Lincoln's whistle-stop tour to the White House and chose to take the oath of office holding the Lincoln Bible. When he visited the Lincoln Memorial with his children ten days before the inauguration, gaggles of media shot images of the family literally standing in the sixteenth president's shadow. To the extent that a single theme emerged in the first days after the election, Lincoln figured prominently within it. One editorial cartoon shows Lincoln's statue giving Obama a double thumbs-up from his perch on the National Mall. Another depicts Lincoln and Martin Luther King Jr. exchanging a high-five on election day. Entrepreneurs played it up as well: One company printed buttons and T-shirts with Obama's image on the Lincoln penny; a publisher rushed into print a book featuring Obama's inaugural address along with Lincoln's first and second inaugurals and the Gettysburg Address.

Some of this is best left not too deeply explored. Lincoln has come down through history as a champion of racial equality, a cause he never actually endorsed. As a young legislator, he paid little attention to issues concerning blacks in Illinois and made no objection when blacks were disfranchised in the state. Nor did he object when Illinois augmented its laws outlawing the transportation of an enslaved black over state lines with a law making it illegal for free blacks to enter the state. His earliest draft of the Emancipation Proclamation contained language stating that the freed blacks would be deported to the most reasonable and convenient locale. On the campaign trail he occasionally made overt declarations of the supremacy of the white race. Obama was, in citing Lincoln, an heir to an ambivalent racial legacy.

Yet their similarities went beyond surface and symbolism. Both men were elected in part because their rivals were divisive figures within their own parties. Lincoln's election had been possible only because Stephen Douglas's authorship of the Kansas-Nebraska Act made him unpopular with both northerners and southerners. Douglas had a tense relationship with outgoing president James Buchanan, disagreeing on the question of slavery in Kansas. Ultimately the Democratic Party was so hopelessly factionalized that it nominated four different candidates for president. John McCain's GOP had only one nominee. But the throngs that came to see Sarah Palin and the groups that came to see him might as well have been two separate parties. McCain's version of Republicanism was nearing its expiration date even as he claimed the party nomination. His conflicted relationship with George W. Bush left him distrusted by that most nebulous but crucial of groups—"the base." His disdain for the excesses of Christian conservatives left him unable to rally that element to his cause, his views were not reliably pro-life, and the business wing of his party (as well as many others outside of it) found him to be lacking on economic matters. His position on immigration policy stood outside the angry version of populist Republicanism. Within a party defined by many subsets, McCain could not act as an adhesive.

During the bitterest stretch of his primary battle with Clinton, Obama referenced Doris Kearns Goodwin's *Team of Rivals*, a history of Lincoln and the cabinet he created from his former adversaries. After the election, as he was establishing his cabinet, Obama appeared to take this creed to heart, tapping Joe Biden, Hillary Clinton, and Bill Richardson, all of whom had competed against him for the nomination. Rumors circulated that John Edwards was to have been the attorney general pick prior to the revelations of his extramarital affair. Lincoln chose William Seward as his secretary of state, Edward Bates as his attorney general, Simon Cameron as his secretary of war, and Salmon Chase as his secretary of the Treasury, all of whom had challenged him for the Republican nomination. But Lincoln's "team of rivals" had been less a matter of getting beyond petty personal rivalries for the national good than nineteenth-century politics as usual. When it came to talent in that era, parties did not have as deep a bench. As historian James Oakes pointed out in the *New York Times*:

> There was nothing new in what Lincoln did. By tradition, presidents-elect reserved a cabinet position, often secretary of state, for the leading rival in their party. John Quincy Adams inaugurated the practice by appointing one of his presidential rivals, Henry Clay, to that post. It was a controversial move in 1824; enemies of Adams denounced the appointment as a corrupt bargain.[56]

Moreover, Lincoln's cabinet was rife with grievances and small-scale bureaucratic skirmishes. The point is, even when speaking of Lincoln, it's possible to take role modeling a tad too far.

Comparing the two men was worthwhile, but not necessarily for the reasons most people thought. During the campaign the Obama team frequently referred to the Bush administration's constitutional excesses. The previous years had seen warrantless wiretaps conducted against American citizens, unsanctioned renditions, torture, and presidential signing statements that seemed to blur the lines between the executive and legislative branches. The Cheney office carved out a unitary niche, effectively separating the vice presidency into its own branch of government. Obama's supporters pointed out that their man's background as a lawyer and a law professor made it less likely that as president he would be prone to such infractions. But this is precisely the kind of action that Lincoln took in the midst of national crisis.

In suspending habeas corpus in 1862, Lincoln not only criminalized interfering with the Union, he criminalized disagreeing with it—at least verbally and in public. Facing a grave threat to the nation's continued existence, Lincoln believed that security had to have a higher priority than freedom. It was a Cheney-esque calculation; or more aptly, Cheney was more Lincolnian in some ways than the young senator from his home state. Consider this situation: A military contractor rakes in huge fees to provide services traditionally performed by the military itself. The public grows concerned about the cozy relationship between the contractor and a member of the executive branch—in fact, the official in question was once in the contractor's employ. Depending upon the era, you are referring either to Halliburton and Dick Cheney or to Abraham Lincoln and the Pinkerton Agency.

Lincoln inherited the White House from a phenomenally weak president. James Buchanan oversaw the secession of seven Confederate states and argued that while he disagreed with it, the Constitution delegated him no authority to prevent it. Lincoln set out to expand the power of the executive branch to the dimensions of the conflict facing the nation. He raised troops without congressional authority, and he allocated funds for the war without following proper legislative channels. As Obama placed his hand on the Bible, quite a different task lay ahead of him. He would take office in the midst of two wars, on the heels of a tremendously, even dangerously powerful president, and would be required to constrict the office to reasonable bounds nonetheless. Presidents alone do not determine how expansive the power of the office should be. But George W. Bush benefited from a Democratic Party that showed little willingness to confront him, partially out of national security concerns echoing down from September 11 and partially out of habit.

Shortly into Obama's first term Senator Arlen Specter wrote a lengthy essay in the *New York Review of Books* stating that he would not allow the presidency to continue along its path toward unchecked authority, a pledge that, while eight years late, might still have been important.

In the seven and a half years since September 11, the United States has witnessed one of the greatest expansions of executive authority in its history, at the expense of the constitutionally mandated separation of powers. President Obama, as only the third sitting senator to be elected president in American history, and the first since John F. Kennedy, may be more likely to respect the separation of powers than President Bush was. But rather than put my faith in any president to restrain the executive branch, I intend to take several concrete steps, which I hope the new president will support.[57]

However, Specter's capacity to act as watchdog was severely curtailed when the eroding Republican base in Pennsylvania forced him to switch parties. As a newly minted Democrat, thankful to be admitted to the caucus, he was hardly in a position to roil the waters.

Ultimately how Obama wields executive authority depends on his character, which is perhaps the essence of the Lincoln comparisons. The will to avoid excess is an aspect of character, whether one is dealing with chocolate or executive orders. Obama may have been deliberately seeking to emulate Lincoln's character. Regardless of the overblown analogies, Lincoln remained the most severely tested of presidents, steering the nation through four years of fratricide. He endured the death of his-ten-year-old son. He was disregarded and criticized even by his closest allies and reviled as the cause of the war. His own commander of Union forces ran against him for president. Inheriting an economy teetering toward depression, an unpopular war in Iraq, and an intractable one in Afghanistan, Obama likely held a regard for Lincoln that ran deeper than policies and proclamations.

Curiously, the word *lash* appears both in Obama's inaugural address and in Lincoln's second inaugural. It is not a standard word for inaugural speeches, it doesn't appear in generations of oratory the way *patriot* and *values* and *equality* register every four years. And Obama is altogether too careful a craftsman of words for that to be coincidental.

Obama:

> For us, they [immigrants] packed up their few worldly possessions and traveled across oceans in search of a new life. For us, they toiled in sweatshops and settled the West, endured the lash of the whip and plowed the hard earth.

Lincoln:

> Fondly do we hope, fervently do we pray, that this mighty scourge of war may speedily pass. Yet if God wills that it continue until all the wealth piled by the bondsman's two hundred and fifty years of unrequited toil shall be sunk, and until every drop of blood drawn with the lash shall be paid by another drawn with the sword, as was said three thousand years ago, so still must be said, "the judgments of the Lord are true and righteous altogether.[58]

It was a masterfully subtle nod, a recognition perhaps that Obama is not Lincoln—nor any other presidential predecessor— but that they are nonetheless bound to a common narrative, lashed, in effect, to the same themes of trial and perseverance, race and progress, turbulence and, inevitably, change.

CHAPTER 8

Where Do We Go from Here?

IN HIS FIRST AT-BAT as a Brooklyn Dodger, Jackie Robinson hit a triple. The details of that day—inning, velocity, attendance in Ebbets Field—are forgotten, dwarfed by the larger narrative, in which a single swing moved Robinson from the athletic realm into the symbolic one. His batting average during his ensuing slump and the fielding percentages that betray his difficulty in adjusting to his new position are ghost data. Only the fact that he was the First is concrete.

A random citizen who heard the crack of Robinson's bat may have understood it as a small glory and a harbinger of grand ones. The people then known as colored heard it as a verification that one of their own can succeed in the white world if given the chance. But a quotient of black people—those who understood segregation as more of a boundary than a barrier—heard in that sound an ambivalent finality. For them it meant the end of the Negro Leagues and the comfort of the community that had sprung up around it.

Robinson made it possible for the world to delight in the majesty of Josh Gibson and Satchel Paige and Hank Aaron. His appearance in a Dodger uniform prefaced a world in which team allegiances were geographic, not racial, in which a white man from Brooklyn and a black man living in Mississippi could equally revere Willie Mays. *Including* means having to share. Robinson's swing altered the balance between the words *black* and *American*, shifted them closer to equilibrium, and forced into existence a subtle new identity. As a First Black, Robinson stood at the cross-currents of history. He more than anyone could testify that change is difficult. If Barack Obama did not empathize more with Jackie Robinson during the course of his campaign, he certainly came to understand him better.

The First Black is always a barometer. The integration of baseball occurred not because Robinson was the first athlete to be worthy of inclusion in the major leagues, but because American society was changing. It is no coincidence that he arrived in the big leagues just two years after the United States defeated Nazi fascism and the entire world had been exposed to the meaning of Hitler's mad racialism.

In Robinson, the Dodgers found a player whose unique combination of talent and temperament would allow him to slip through the cracks in Jim Crow. Unspoken rules come with being a First Black. Robinson became one of many black diplomats dispatched to the white world. As such, he was required to possess supernatural reserves of grace in the face of hostility and the Zen-like self-possession otherwise known as cool.

A common bond connects Robinson's approach to baseball to Obama's brand of politics.

If baseball is a microcosm for American society, there's something to be said for this relationship between Robinson and Obama. We are more than clear about what is required of anyone cast in the role of First Black. Black people have replicated Robinson's example on a small scale with individual entries into previously all-white arenas: the prep school, the boardroom, the manicured subdivision. Breaching those worlds required the First Blacks, more often than not, to explain the black world to their white peers, the object of a racial poll in which the sample size is a single individual. Prior to the 2008 election Americans may have believed that First Black status was an antiquated concept. (Four decades after the civil rights movement ended America has plenty of Only Blacks but rarely any more First Blacks.)

Obama's Jackie Robinson moment came in Iowa, as millions of people recognized that the parameters had shifted unpredictably and dramatically. And with it came the same tide of glory and ambivalence that Robinson inspired in 1947. Nostalgia is a powerful force, and few of us negotiate change with complete grace. Some of the fiercest opposition to the *Brown v. Board of Education* decision was found within the black community. The writer Zora Neale Hurston denounced the ruling as a bitter statement that a black-only world could not be the equal of a white one. Principals of all-black schools derided the NAACP's efforts, believing that they would never be allowed to steward integrated schools and that the *Brown* decision would leave them unemployed. Parents fretted at the prospect of launching their children out of the protective enclave that generations of black people had molded from Jim Crow and into the hostile white world. More fundamentally, integration posed challenges to who black people in this country understood themselves to be.

The old unspoken rules still apply. Obama is performing a high-wire act with the pitfalls of race surrounding him. Like all such acrobatics, his has only a microscopic margin for error. He must reassure suspicious whites, while not appearing to be unduly concerned about reassuring whites. The task is nearly impossible. The backlash against Obama's Father's Day demand that black men be responsible parents was driven not by disagreement with those sentiments but by fear that Obama had tilted too far toward whites—and their perceptions of black irresponsibility.

Just prior to the Democratic convention, conservative commentary went hypertensive at the prospect that Colin Powell would endorse Barack Obama. He had, after all, praised Obama in the preceding months. In truth Powell's praise likely had less to do with partisan politics than with the fact that the First

Black secretary of state understood better than most the waters Obama was attempting to navigate. Many suspected that Powell had remained with the Bush administration, despite his contempt for its Iraq policy, because of the pressure to succeed as a Black First. Unlike William Jennings Bryan or Caspar Weinberger, secretaries of state who resigned in protest of the administrations they served, Powell would have faced the barb that a black man could not handle the pressure of the position.

When Powell did endorse Obama, with uncommon grace and eloquence, some predictably missed this context entirely and believed, as Rush Limbaugh so ineptly put it, that "this is about race."

JAMES BALDWIN ONCE OBSERVED that black leaders have traditionally had to implore whites to hurry up while begging blacks to wait. As president, Obama is so far outside the traditional concept of a "black leader" as to require a redefinition of the term. But the sense among African Americans that this society needs to "hurry up" remains constant.

The days leading to inauguration were pockmarked by signs of progress and how far we had yet to go. As a black man planned to assume the most powerful office in the world, three black men were shot by police in the first eight days of 2009, two of them fatally; two of them unarmed. The third had a license to carry the weapon found on his body. In Oakland twenty-two-year-old Oscar Grant was shot while prone and completely defenseless on the pavement of a BART station. In New Orleans, Adolph Grimes, also twenty-two, was shot fourteen times in front of his grandmother's house. Police reported that he shot at them first, but that could not explain why twelve of their bullets hit him in the back. Houston police shot twenty-three-year-old Robbie Tolan in his own driveway, after assuming that the car he drove with friends was stolen. As he lay in a hospital bed, his father told media: If these had been white kids, it would not have happened.

A fragmentary calculus goes into deciding who is a threat and who isn't; when to pull the trigger, and when to issue a warning. Cops go to work each day with a realistic expectation that they may not return home; but black men pay taxes to fund public servants who are disproportionately prone to kill us. It happens frequently enough that the events following those shootings adhere to a bitterly cliché script.

Outraged activists pour into the streets demanding the prosecution of the cops for murder and an enhanced civilian review board. The police bureaucracy stonewalls, while PBA lawyers work up schemes for plausible deniability. The media spin out two weeks' worth of it's-a-shame stories: the shot of the yellow police tape; the interview with the family; the brief update on the funeral; the nondescript statement from the chief of police. The cycle ends with an even smaller note about the internal review clearing all officers of wrongdoing (unless the decision sparks a riot).

It all seemed so . . . pre-Obama.

During the spring of 2008 a judge acquitted four officers of any wrongdoing in the fatal shooting of Sean Bell: On what was to have been his wedding day, the unarmed Bell had been the target of fifty bullets. In response to the acquittal, candidate Obama called for calm and respect for the law, which struck some as inordinately even-handed in the face of an outrage. In the context of a presidential campaign, it made sense—no presidential candidate would've gone close to the postverdict demonstrations, but then only a black candidate would have been expected to. In the midst of the 1992 campaign, when the Los Angeles riots took place, Bill Clinton and George H. W. Bush fumbled around about the issue momentarily and then went back to debating the economy, and no one noticed. In 1960 John F. Kennedy scored tremendous points just by calling Coretta Scott King and pulling some levers to get Dr. King released from jail—precisely because no one would expect a politician to get involved in that kind of firestorm. But Obama's response to Sean Bell highlighted the pitfall of his brand of politics. Race has a way of dragging us all to the lowest denominator. The Achilles' heel of the "postracial" politician—to the extent that such a thing exists—is that there are consistent, clockwork moments of racial outrage that level-headed appeals for calm simply can't address.

That lesson was brought home again early in the administration, when Harvard professor Henry Louis Gates Jr. was arrested in his own home after an officer concluded that he was not attempting to break into the house. Obama, uncharacteristically intemperate, declared that the officer had "acted stupidly"—and those words became the basis for a national feeding frenzy. In the end, a single white police officer made a bogus arrest and received an apology from the president of the United States and an invitation to the White House for beer. Some wondered if Gates might have fared better by calling on Al Sharpton. Obama changed the nature of black leadership long before he arrived at 1600 Pennsylvania Avenue, but these kinds of flashpoints will always provide an opening for a man with a bullhorn.

There is a subtle but crucial difference between being above race and beyond it. "Postracial politics" was always based on the paradoxical assumption that leadership can exist outside the currents that affect the people they are leading.

Over the course of his early months in office a pattern began to emerge. As president of the United States, not just of one ethnic bloc within it, Obama sought to move the entire nation forward. This meant giving most of his attention to the economy, health care, and the wars abroad—the grand concerns affecting all. When he spoke to Tavis Smiley's State of the Black Union gathering in February 2009, he placed the economic concerns of black America in the context of the broader turbulence that was affecting pocketbooks across the country. Just after the election, Barbara Lee, the head of the Congressional Black Caucus, remarked that they did not expect its relationship with Obama to be different from that with any other president. This was politics—assuring the public that the president would not be beholden to a particular constituency. But the statement was—or should have been—wrong: Obama was formerly a member of the Congressional Black Caucus, and African Americans represent a full quarter of his electorate. If Lee was right, then it was alarming.

But while Obama's election changed the relationship of blacks to America, it didn't immediately change the realities. In early summer of his first year in office, unemployment hung at 9.5 percent nationally; in some black communities that rate was doubled. Even the New Deal had shown that a program of national recovery did not automatically assist all portions of the country equally. At some crucial points Obama would have to behave as the black president, not to the exclusion of his other assignments but surely in addition to them.[59]

As THE OLD racial meanings fell away so publicly, more confusion and awkwardness emerged. GQ published a four-thousand-word piece about a white writer's quest to find a black friend. New York ran a clubfooted attempt to explain the racial politics of the Obama marriage, in which the writer pondered whether Barack used the word *nigger* at black campaign events. Cable news generated enough racial backwardness—"terrorist fist jab" and the like—to warrant an encyclopedia of bad judgments that amounted to an indictment of the postracial fantasy. The historian David Levering Lewis told me after the election, "Of course race mattered in this election—it just happened to matter in a good way." The fact that we devoted hundreds of media hours to discussing whether race still mattered was evidence that it did.[60]

Amid the flurry of self-congratulation about the novelty of 2008, history went unnoticed. In 1870 the Fifteenth Amendment granted the right to vote to African-American men. This meant that African Americans had been voting for presidential candidates of another race for 138 years before white Americans opted to do the same. In short, blacks had been voting for whites

for as long as we've been voting. Those truths made the hallelu-
jahs sound somewhat hollow. Reporter Jonathan Kaufmann of
the *Wall Street Journal* observed that black and white college
students attended Obama rallies and campaign events, then
went back to their largely segregated social lives on campus.
People seemed able to express faith in Obama's potential and yet
remained cynical about racial prospects. Though polls later
showed new levels of African American optimism about racial
progress, the election brought complex, even frustrating transi-
tional moments.

Nor did black America hold answers to all the questions
about the new landscape of race. Somewhere in the long stretches
of the summer, the dueling updates and the vendors selling shirts
picturing Obama with Martin, Malcolm, and Mandela, it occurred to me that many black people had it wrong. In a moment
of blockheaded fervor, the rapper Ludacris recorded a song in
support of Obama in which he rhymed about "painting the White
House black." Not long afterward Spike Lee hailed Obama's
ascension as the start of a "chocolate city" effect, dusting off the
term African Americans had used to describe our growing urban electoral power in the 1970s. Both were wrong about what
Barack Obama represents. At that point I wondered if blacks
were going to embrace Obama without embracing the multihued
broad coalition he necessarily represented.

In August 2008, at the opening of the new Obama office in
midtown Atlanta, a deejay was spinning Parliament Funkadelic
classics at a festive late-summer barbecue. A man in the parking
lot proudly sported a T-shirt with images of Martin Luther
King Jr. and Barack Obama. Above Dr. King were the words
"The Dreamer" and below Obama "The Dream." It was the
first of many times I would see that particular T-shirt.

I felt a twinge of concern. No living politician could stand
a chance when measured against a martyred visionary. Martin
Luther King Jr. wouldn't even want to be compared to Martin
Luther King Jr. He was vested by a moral mandate, one that stood
at odds with the political structure of his time. Had he been a

politician, he would have given Lyndon Johnson his loyalty (or at least owed him a political debt) for signing the Civil and Voting Rights acts. Instead Dr. King criticized LBJ for escalating the nation's involvement in Vietnam. King retained his moral currency, but his criticism depressed his political stock. King's stand was placed in even greater contrast by the fact that Obama had been accused over the course of the summer of eschewing moral stands and tacking to the center for political expediency.

But another part of me, the thirty-eight-year-old black man, knew exactly where that man was coming from and why he wore the shirt with such obvious pride. *Barack* means "blessed" in Swahili, but in the language of black America his name rapidly came to mean "the content of our character." Obama has been inducted into that pantheon of glory that black people have turned to time and again to keep the dogs of despair at bay. But the achievements of Joe Louis and Jesse Owens, of Muhammad Ali and Jack Johnson, were glimmering citations of black brilliance in the face of white hostility. Barack Obama denotes a different, maybe even novel type of heroism. He belongs to a broader constituency than any African American who preceded him. Black America is, on levels grand and minute, a stakeholder in his success, but so are the millions of white voters who supported him during the election.

In July 2007, when he was still trailing Clinton among black voters, Obama addressed the National Association of Black Journalists and announced that it was time for African Americans to move beyond the reflexive suspicion of any black person who is admired by whites. Given Ludacris's sophomoric declarations about "painting the White House black," it was clear that we were all feeling our way into this new era.

We were all frantically trying to retrofit a new reality into our old assumptions. I, at least, had thought that we would not see a black president until the society had uniformly moved forward, until black incarceration was no longer the leading growth industry, until we were no longer disproportionately impoverished and locked out of the health care system. But as a historian, I should have known better. If anything, lopsided history is the rule, not the exception. As the first black senators and governors took office during Reconstruction, southern devotees of the Lost Cause were furiously working to perfect new forms of slavery. The first successful black businesses were launched as lynching became a perverse form of recreation in the South. Ralph Bunche won a Nobel Prize at a time when he would not have been allowed to vote in many states.

So what *does* it mean to live in a country where 64 million people voted to make a black man a president? Does it hail the beginning of a new kind of country, one that has made good on its self-professed exceptionalism? Does it represent the last best push of a human rights movement that over time and centuries wore down bigotry the way water passes through stone? What does it mean to have a black man as president when nearly a million other black men are incarcerated? When over a third of black children live below the poverty line? When nearly half the HIV deaths in this country are African American?

In 2002 reporters asked Denzel Washington what it meant for three African Americans to be in contention for Academy Awards in the same year. He replied, "It means that three African Americans are in contention for Academy Awards in the same year." I am tempted to answer the question about the meaning of a black presidency with the same terms: It means that the president is black. And anything beyond that will be left for time to tell.

THOUGH I WOULD NOT HAVE admitted it at the time, in some ways the nomination of Barack Obama was an anticlimax. The Democratic Party orchestrated the elaborate flea-flicker pass between delegations, allowing Hillary Clinton to formally put Obama's name into nomination. But the process itself was more akin to applying for a driver's license than changing the direction of history. That is, until the next morning. I caught the tail end of a prayer breakfast at the convention center. Celebrities filtered past reporters virtually unnoticed, and clergymen offered long-winded meditations on the meaning of Obama. All were still trying to figure it out. It was fitting that eighty-six-year-old Reverend Joseph Lowery closed the event. He spoke a few words and then requested that the people in attendance stand, link arms, and sing "We Shall Overcome." The song had begun to show its seams years earlier. We take its lyrics for granted; over the years it became such a mainstay of civil rights commemorations and anniversaries that its actual intent faded into the background. But a strange thing happened in Denver. The song's meaning changed in ways that were both immediate and profound. Few if any of the five hundred people in that room made it through the first chorus before the tears began streaming.

For reasons that are both deeply personal and thoroughly common, I thought about my father at that point. He passed on seventeen years earlier. Willie Lee Cobb was born in a stoplight town called Hazelhurst, Georgia, in 1920. He was what they would call corn-fed, six foot three and well muscled. He was given to flights of imagination that he disguised as biography—outsize tales of his days as a boxer, a baseball player, an itinerant colored man surveying the boundaries of the Jim Crow world. His stories were a delight to his children, but imagination and biography both stopped cold at the subject of his Georgia roots. I asked him once about what life was like when he was a child, and he offered dry words: No reason to go talking about all that. Memory, like schools, water fountains, and train cars, has its own brutal boundaries.

Here are the things not worth talking about: In 1929 a white man came to my grandmother's house to evict her. She had no money and no job. The man looked over at my father, quietly protective of his mother and much bigger than his nine years would suggest. His offer: You send that boy on out to my field, and I'll let him work "till he pays off the money you owe." That was my father's last day as a child, the boundary between the world of school and that of work. He finished the third grade.

I thought of him as we sang and of all those others who had not lived to see this day and pondered their absence, because this was about them, really.

It was beyond imagining that one of their line would knock on doors in stoplight South Carolina towns, canvassing for a black presidential candidate. Or that eight months after that he would represent their native state of Georgia and help place that candidate's name into nomination. There were millions of individual trajectories inside that song, biographies converging at a single point, with a singular hope of seeing a black man place his hand on a Bible held by his wife and take an oath.

On the eve of the election I got a late-night haircut at a twenty-four-hour barbershop because I had a media appearance early the following morning. When I asked about the election, I learned that none of the six men working there was even registered to vote. One made a crude sexual remark about Sarah Palin. A few of them were clearly high. It was a sobering moment.

The day after the election I drove past Capitol View Elementary School, which displayed a flashing sign that read "Barack Obama, Barack Obama, Barack Obama." The principal wanted to ensure that the new president's name was the first thing her students saw that morning. The school sits in one of the worst zip codes in Atlanta in terms of crime, poverty, and foreclosures. Its windows look down upon the neglected shell that once housed a fried chicken joint. Prostitutes work the corner directly across the street from the building. Yet it is one of the best schools in the city. Its students routinely score in the top ranks on standardized tests. The wide, clean hallways were filled with excited, bright-eyed young children.

Those two lopsided moments managed to encapsulate the experience of 2008 in black America. Those of us who are inclined to push forward are taking Barack Obama as inspiration. Some of us have scarcely noticed him at all. This was the meaning of progress.

We are in a place more asymmetrical than any since the days when some of us were slave and some were free. It's January 20, 2009. Some of us live in the White House, some of us live on the street. Most of us are somewhere in between and still trying to decipher the meaning of our times. Joseph Lowery was wise to bring us back to that song at the convention. And the song was correct. We *shall* overcome.

Just not all at the same time.

Coda

In July 2009 Barack Obama recognized yet another alignment of history: the convention celebrating the one hundredth anniversary of the NAACP's founding. He offered them a rousing congratulatory speech, echoing the ones he'd delivered in Selma and South Carolina. His cadence and rhythm took on tones of the black church as he spoke about the travails of the past and the determination that saw us through them, sounding in some ways like the pastor-in-chief. Many politicians have felt compelled to visit the black church; Barack Obama's unique gift was his ability to turn other environments into the black church. On some level this is what politicians do—communicate with people in their native tongue. In this instance it was more complicated.

He bluntly testified to the continued need for the NAACP and the recalcitrance of racism despite his election. And in a moving personal admission he said that he often saw black men on street corners and thought to himself, "There but for the grace of God go I." This was a man who campaigned on a promise to tell people things they didn't necessarily want to hear. True to his word, he chided the black community, targeting familiar shortcomings: fatherless children, high dropout rates, and irresponsibility. He had employed such tactics in his own life; he could say these things because he was asking of this community no more than he had already asked of himself.

The speech conjured dueling emotions. He was no longer an

activist, in the sense he had once been. Nor was he part of a prestigious legislative body where power is diffused among ninety-nine other members. He was the president of the United States. He was now someone of whom the young community organizer in Chicago would have been skeptical, simply because compromise is a hallmark of politics. The young Obama would have taken note of a black president but thought about him mostly in terms of his community's particular interests. The speech was also a needed reminder that, history aside, Obama will ultimately be measured by what he does—not what he means.

I was amused at the thought that someone as intimately familiar with the rites and ways of the black church had found his way to the White House (though Bill Clinton had arguably performed that role before Obama). But the scene was also troubling to the extent that preachers are seldom questioned, rarely held accountable, and can often fulfill their job requirements simply by making people feel good. Pastors hold their people accountable; presidents must be accountable to their people. He could not just list a litany of ills in the black community unless he also listed the ways in which his office had targeted them— even as he urged black people to dig deeper, strive harder, and push forward. Other currents had begun to take shape by July. Five months into his term the metaphors that had accumulated like lint on a black sweater during the campaign season had begun to shift. Gone was the *tabula rasa* symbol of post-partisanship, the Lucite candidate who could reflect an entire spectrum of ideas and aspirations. In his place was a figure that inspired nearly Clintonian levels of division and distrust. The first hints of this surfaced during the campaign—the fevered accusations that Obama was a radical Muslim, the McCain rallies where storm clouds of paranoia began to gather. But by the following summer, they were altogether something different. Just twelve days after the NAACP speech, Fox News host Glenn Beck declared on-air that the biracial president "has a deep-seated hatred for white people," a statement that required a nearly hallucinatory commitment to avoiding evidence to the contrary.

Yet Beck was not alone in his delusions. The first months of Obama's term saw a drumbeat of overwrought suspicions: Tea Party rallies where the administration was compared to the tyranny of King George III, "Birthers" assailing the public with the false claim that Obama was not an American citizen, town hall meetings where armed citizens shouted about government plans to create "death panels" and kill the elderly. A cavalry of cranks marching into the conspiratorial ethers.

That fearful imagination and the demonstrations it inspired became a sort of object lesson about symbolism—that just as Obama could be made to represent all manner of progressive ambitions during the campaign, there was nearly equal elasticity for those who wished to paint him as the embodiment of all that was wrong with America. Only in that context could the random, feuding labels assigned to him—Marxist, fascist, Muslim, socialist, black nationalist, foreigner—even begin to be deciphered.

The rising temperature on the right became most apparent in September for two reasons: President Obama offered an inspirational speech to the nation's young people as they returned to school, and addressed a joint session of Congress about the importance of health care reform. In an act of imponderable hostility, some parents withheld consent for the president of the United States to encourage their children to study hard. Critics on the right alleged he was attempting to indoctrinate America's children. That same hostility surfaced in the joint congressional session. In response to Obama's statement that the proposed health care legislation would not extend coverage to illegal immigrants, Representative Joe Wilson of South Carolina interrupted Obama's speech to shout, "You lie!"

When Jimmy Carter entered the fray, stating the obvious—that much of this hostility derived from the refusal of many Americans to accept the reality of an African American president—the Obama administration found itself in the awkward position of denying the point. Press Secretary Robert Gibbs appeared on CNN shortly after the statement and deflected Carter's charge, saying, "I don't think the president believes that people are upset because of the color of his skin. I think people are upset because on Monday we celebrate the anniversary of the Lehman Brothers collapse that caused a financial catastrophe unlike anything we've ever seen." On some level both men were correct, though not for the reason Gibbs offered.

In 1965, historian Richard Hofstadter published *The Paranoid Style in American Politics*, in which he pointed out that a tradition of irrational fear stretched back to the founding days of the republic when Americans suspected a secret cabal of Tories would steal their hard-won liberty. At various times the public has feared that their freedom would be subverted by clandestine sects of Freemasons, Catholics, corporate barons, anarchists, socialists, and communists. An updated version of the list would include radical Islamic terrorists. The menace these various isms present is always total, always fatal to the most cherished values, always present, and always invisible. Thus a corresponding tradition of groups, alliances, or sects, each devoted to defeating this surreptitious evil.

By inclination, these movements are most energized during Democratic presidencies (although, as Hofstadter pointed out, a similar if less prominent strand of paranoia exists among the left). During Roosevelt's presidency the reactionary radio host Father Coughlin warned the nation of blossoming socialism; Senator Joseph McCarthy charged Truman's administration with harboring communists. John F. Kennedy's term gave rise to the John Birch Society and Bill Clinton's years coincided with the rise of right-wing militias whose contempt for government found expression in Timothy McVeigh's 1995 bombing of the Alfred P. Murrah office building in Oklahoma City. On some level this paranoia—and the pandering it inspires within the GOP—during Obama's presidency is a predictable outgrowth of this tradition. Yet Carter was not wrong. During the "9/12" rallies of September 2009, protestors carried images depicting Obama as a racial caricature: an unclad African with a bone driven through his nose.

The velocity at which the glimmering moment in history

corroded into the old racial quagmire—the half-life of civic goodwill—mocked the idealism of the campaign era. It was the most colossal of ironies that whites took to the streets to protest the threat to their freedom posed by a black president—in a country where blacks spent 266 years as slaves. The paranoid shoe, if anything, belonged on the other foot.

The meaning of racial progress, once as clear as the skies on that fall night in Grant Park, became opaque, complex. In December 2009, nearly one year after Barack Obama was sworn in as president, the *New York Times* ran a story with the headline "In Job Hunt, College Degree Can't Close Racial Gap." The article pointed out that

> there is ample evidence that racial inequities remain when it comes to employment. Black joblessness . . . as the recession has dragged on, has been even more pronounced for those with college degrees, compared with those without. Education, it seems, does not level the playing field—in fact, it appears to have made it more uneven. College-educated black men, especially, have struggled relative to their white counterparts in this downturn, according to figures from the Bureau of Labor Statistics. The unemployment rate for black male college graduates 25 and older in 2009 has been nearly twice that of white male college graduates—8.4 percent compared with 4.4 percent.[62]

These, it seemed, were sentences suited for the old era, artifacts of 2008 wrested into the present. Or, more likely, yet another indicator of the paradox, the opportunity gap that is both highlighted and defined by the election of a black president. Those disparate realities ignited an autumn brush fire between the White House and the Congressional Black Caucus as the latter threatened to vote against economic recovery provisions of the Obama administration that did not do more to target the needs of poor black communities. For his part, Obama responded as he had during the campaign—that black problems existed in concert with bigger American problems and his job was to lift the nation as a whole. In short, there would be no Adjective-Americans in his administration, at least not on the level of policy. This was change. But it was hard to call it progress.

It will fall to future observers to ponder if Barack Obama's race made him less capable of assisting the black community and whether the balance of his presidency tilts more toward symbolic or tangible gains.

This much is clear: We live our lives in literal terms, not metaphorical ones. And perhaps that is the point Obama attempted to make in the NAACP speech: He is a president, not an antidote. We are not postracial; we are not postpartisan. We are American, with all the unwieldy, contradictory implications of that identity. The paradoxes are ours to assume; Barack Obama is simply a man and a president. His election is best understood as a passing respite, a brief moment of rest before it falls to us to once again turn our shoulder to the wheel of history.

Acknowledgments

This book began in the spring of 2007, when I attended an Obama rally at Georgia Tech. I was skeptical about the candidate and even more skeptical about his prospects. But even at that early juncture the campaign was attracting large crowds to its rallies. In this instance that crowd included a small knot of Kenyan students who held up a sign greeting the senator. This was also the first time the Reverend Joseph Lowery spoke on behalf of Obama. He delivered a magnificent benediction, as energetic and inspiring an introduction as anyone running for president could hope for.

I appreciated the reverend's words, but my eyebrow remained raised regarding Obama. Then within the first twenty seconds on the stage, he won my vote. He walked out to thundering applause and promptly said "Jambo" to the Kenyan delegation. I liked the idea of a president who knew the traditional Swahili greeting. This was no multicultural litmus test that an upstart managed to pass, it was part of a much broader concern that defined the previous eight years. Among his numerous other shortcomings, perhaps the most egregious flaw of George W. Bush and those who surrounded him was an inability to see the rest of the world, much less understand how they perceived their own lives, their interests, and their place on our small crowded planet. I thought someone who recognized those Kenyan students would also recognize other people and might be a remedy to the declining global regard for the United States. Not that he had a three-legged dog's chance of winning, I thought. I was fully prepared to vote for him simply to make a point.

I did vote for him, in the primaries, as a delegate, and during the general election, and my point was also being made by young voters and older ones, blacks, Latinos, and even a sizable number of "hard-working white folk." This book tells part of that story from my perspective as both a participant and an observer. It would not have been possible without the input, encouragement, and assistance of the many smart, supportive people I'm fortunate to have in my life.

My agent, Charlotte Sheedy, believed in this project when it was simply an eight-hundred-word op-ed in the pages of the *Washington Post*. She has been the definition of the word *support* and an invaluable sounding board. (I hope introducing her to sweet potato pancakes offers some small measure of my gratitude.) My editors, George Gibson and Jackie Johnson, were patient, insightful, and remarkably calm when I essentially rewrote this project to reflect my views on a rapidly changing subject. I'm thankful for their support as well.

My mother, Mary Cobb, managed to ask me about the book when I needed to be asked and ignored the subject when I needed it to be ignored. Kat Brown provided wit, encouragement, and, most important, quiet space as I worked on the final section of the book. Lonnae O'Neal Parker and Ralph Parker generously opened their home for a "writer's lock-in," where I wrote part of the book. Jen Brea, who seemed to parachute into Nairobi, out of random sky, introduced me to restaurants, parks, and most crucially, the People's Parliament. Her intellect and insight exceed her years, and I eagerly anticipate reading her own books in the near future. I was also the beneficiary of conversations that helped me think through a topic that seemed to grow more complex and amazing at hourly intervals. I appreciate my exchanges with Andra Gillespie, Ta-Nehisi Coates, Natalie Moore, Melissa Harris-Lacewell, Stanley Crouch, Lester Spence, Danyel Smith, Rob Kenner, Natalie Hopkinson, Lynette Clemetson, Mikael Moore, and Jack White.

I'm indebted to my fellow delegates, who are too many to

mention, but especially to the Five for Five slate: Camara Jones, Deidre Barrett-England, Emily Schunior, and Gregg Bossen. Also Kimberlyn Carter, James Beverly, Mary Long, Preston Harden, Jerry Riley, and Julie Borders. Saaret Yosef and Terence Samuel were great resources as I wrote the "Delegate" blog for Theroot.com during the Democratic National Convention.

Several people took time out of their schedules to sit for interviews, which proved invaluable. My thanks go to Eric Easter, Anton Gunn, Dr. Johnetta B. Cole, Reverend Jesse Jackson, Representative Jesse Jackson Jr., Reverend Joseph Lowery, Representative John Lewis, Tharon Johnson, Mayor Shirley Franklin, Lisa Borders, Biko Baker, Representative Maxine Waters, Ron Walters, Kevin Powell, Malaika Moses, Reverend Raphael Wurnock, and David Banner.

A general shout-out goes to the friends who supported this project and me despite my occasional episodes of grump: Lisa Brown and the Brown family, Mark and Carolyn Mason, Mali Fleming, Don and Deb Sinkfield, Carley Lester, Errin Haines, Christy Nixon, Alita Anderson, Andie Davis, Rhea Combs, Thomas Breeze, Jodine Dorce, Ayoka Chenzira, Tim Richardson, Modupe Agueh, Haj, Tyrone M. Mitchell, Sharon Woodley, Renee Holtz, Indra Tobias, Ashley Fantz, Shaila Dewan, Faith Carmichael, and Lyle Harris.

Additional thanks to Jane Malloy, Andrew Lee, Kim Pearson, Daryl Scott, Rudolph Byrd, Mark Naison, Khalil and Stephanie Muhammad, Stephanie and Charles Wright, Tiffany Gill, Tonya Bolden, Warren Lee, Valerie, Natasha, William, and TJ Foster, Tymel Bester (who will become a great lawyer some day), Kenny and Joy Carroll, Renegade, Kamasi Hill, Matthew, Alexis, and Reggie Williams, Alejandro Bodipo-Memba, Travis Ray, Grace Ali, Laurel Beatty, Matt Bigg, Marti Adams, Davey D, Fahamu Pecou, Fred Hanna, Lasana Hotep, Matthew Whitaker, Walter Kimbrough, Joan Morgan, Mitzi Miller, Sharon Sanders, Hiewet Senghor, James Steele, Chandra Thomas, Mike Williams, Divine and Sherese Bender, Loren and Tawkiyah Harris, Al Young, and Shelly Wynter.

Also my colleagues at Spelman College: Dalila DeSousa, Azaria Mbughuni, Beverly Guy Sheftall, James Gillam, Margery Ganz, Kathleen Philips-Lewis, and Cynthia Neal Spence, as well as President Beverly Daniel Tatum and Provost Johnella Butler. I was saved from my own logistical shortcomings more than once by Nicole Smith, and she has my gratitude.

I offer one last note of thanks to my aunt Ann Adams and my cousins Reverend Frank Cobb, Joanne Townsend Gaines, Carla Worthy, Michael McButts, James Johnson, Kim Johnson, and Avery Carter. Precious Green provided invaluable support during my delegate campaign and I'm certain I would not have won without her. Nandi A. Wright, of course, remains my favorite person and a source of inspiration.

Notes

1. Barack and Michelle Obama, interview by Steve Kroft, *60 Minutes*, February 9, 2007.
2. Reverend Joseph Lowery, interview by author, April 2008.
3. Nate Silver told this story at the University of Chicago's conference on the election in November 2008. Journalist Stephanie Ramage of Atlanta's *Sunday Paper* reported hearing an off-the-cuff conversation along these lines, as did Errin Haines in a piece published by AP ahead of the Michigan primary.
4. Barack Obama, *The Audacity of Hope: Thoughts on Reclaiming the American Dream* (New York: Crown, 2006), p. 11.
5. Barack Obama, *Dreams from My Father: A Story of Race and Inheritance* (New York: Three River Press, 2004), p. 44.
6. Joan Morgan, interview by author, May 2, 2009.
7. Ibid.; Sara Rimer and Karen Arenson, "Top Colleges Take More Blacks, But Which Ones?" *New York Times*, June 24, 2004.
8. Frederick Douglass, "What to the Slave Is the Fourth of July?" in Deidre Mullane, ed., *Crossing the Danger Water: Three Hundred Years of African-American Writing* (New York: Anchor, 1993), p. 160.
9. James Baldwin, *The Evidence of Things Not Seen* (New York: Owl Books, 1995).
10. "An Open Letter to Jodi Kantor from Rev. Jeremiah Wright," *New York Times*, March 11, 2007.
11. Susan Jones, ed., *Barack Obama: Words That Inspired a Nation* (New York: Fall River, 2009), pp. 101–02.
12. Bakari Kitwana, "Wright, Obama Engaged in Generational Conflict," Newsmax.com, May 12, 2008.

13. Louis's comments appeared in his *New York Daily News* column, April 29, 2008.

14. E-mails to author in response to Jelani Cobb, "As Obama Rises, Old Guard Civil Rights Leaders Scowl," *Washington Post*, B1, January 13, 2008.

15. Richard Muhammad and Askia Muhammad, "Senator Barack Obama's Big Win: Is America changing her attitude?" January 14, 2008, http://www.finalcall.com/artman/publish/article_4285.shtml.

16. Roddie Burris, "Jackson Slams Obama for 'Acting White,'" *The State*, September 19, 2007.

17. "Jesse Jackson; Most Democratic Candidates Ignoring Black Voters," *Chicago Sun-Times*, November 27, 2007.

18. Jesse Jackson Jr., "You're Wrong About Obama, Dad," *Chicago Sun-Times*, December 2, 2007.

19. Jesse Jackson Jr., interview by author, May 2008.

20. David Murray, e-mail to author, July 10, 2008.

21. James Hirsen, "Rapper Slams Jackson Over Obama Insults," NewsMax.com, July 14, 2008. Ludacris skewered Jackson on "Politics as Usual," a track released on a mixtape during the summer of 2008.

22. Jesse Jackson Jr., press release, July 9, 2008.

23. Ron Walters, interview by author, June 2008; Jesse Jackson Jr., interview by author, May 2008.

24. Walters interview, June 2008.

25. Marshall Frady, *Jesse: The Life and Pilgrimage of Jesse Jackson* (New York: Random House, 1996), p. 343.

26. Mark Anthony Neal, NewsMax.com, May 2008.

27. Jesse Jackson, "1988 Democratic National Convention Speech," Americanrhetoric.com.

28. Eric Easter, "What Jesse Said," EbonyJet.com, July 10, 2008; Stanley Crouch, "Ready on My Mind," in *Notes of a Hanging Judge* (New York: Oxford University Press, 1991).

29. Jesse Jackson, "1984 Democratic National Convention Speech," Americanrhetoric.com.

30. In August 2006, in response to a question about Walmart's impact upon mom-and-pop establishments, Young remarked that the black community had been exploited consecutively by Jewish, Arab, and Korean retailers. The resulting controversy led to calls for his resignation.

31. Debra Dickerson, "Colorblind," Salon.com, January 22, 2007.

32. Rachel Swarns and Regina Pacifici, "So Far Obama Can't Take Black Vote for Granted," *New York Times*, February 2, 2007.

33. In February 2007 a group of genealogy researchers pointed out that an ancestor of Sharpton's had been held in bondage by the ancestors of Strom Thurmond. *Washington Post*, February 26, 2007, p. A1.

34. "Selma Voting Rights March Commemoration," March 4, 2007, BarackObama.com.

35. Ta-Nehisi Coates, "The Irrelevant Rev. Sharpton," *Washington Post*, October 28, 2007.

36. Stephanie Mencimer, "Civil Rights Groups Defending Predatory Lenders: Priceless," *Mother Jones*, August 1, 2008; Linda Saab, "Black Spokesman Title Still Up for Grabs," Gallup.com, July 14, 2008.

37. On March 29, 2008, Sheila Jackson Lee arrived at the delegate caucus in her home district. A videotape caught the sounds of boos as she arrived and was later uploaded onto YouTube.com. It became a centerpiece in debates about whether support for Clinton would make black legislators vulnerable.

38. Gloria Steinem, "Women Are Never Frontrunners," *New York Times*, January 8, 2008.

39. Ta-Nehisi Coates, "A Deeper Black," *Nation*, May 1, 2008.

40. Melissa Harris-Lacewell, "Who Died and Made Tavis King?" Theroot.com, February 15, 2008.

41. Reverend Joseph Lowery, interview by author, April 2008.

42. "In South, Democrats' Tactics May Change Political Game," *Wall Street Journal*, January 23, 2008, p. A1.

43. Anton Gunn, interview by author, June 27, 2008.

44. Christopher Cooper, Valerie Bauerlein, and Corey Dade, "In South, Democrats' Tactics May Change Political Game," *Wall Street Journal*, January 23, 2008.

45. Maxine Waters, interview by author, June 2008.

46. Johnetta Cole, interview by author, June 2008.

47. Barack Obama, "Victory Speech in South Carolina," transcript from CNN.com.

48. Malaika Moses Mitchell, interview by author, June 2008; John Lewis, interview by author, July 2008.

49. The conflict between Booker and James was chronicled in Marshall Curry's documentary *Streetfight*, which shows scenes of harassment of Booker supporters, shakedowns for campaign

contributions, and public questioning of Booker's racial background and allegiances.

50. Obama, *Dreams from My Father*, p. 161.

51. "Fact Sheet on Black America 2008," *Journal of Blacks in Higher Education*, JBHE.com.

52. David Banner, interview by author, July 2008.

53. Barack Obama, speech at Howard University, September 28, 2007, BarackObama.com.

54. Bakari Kitwana, interview by author, July 2008.

55. Equal Employment Opportunity Commission, press release, April 16, 2008.

56. James Oakes, "What's So Special About a Team of Rivals?" *New York Times*, November 19, 2008.

57. Arlen Specter, "The Need to Roll Back Presidential Power Grabs," *New York Review of Books*, May 14, 2009.

58. Barack Obama, *The Inaugural Address, 2009* (New York: Penguin Books, 2009), pp. 6, 20.

59. The *New York Times* observed that the recession hit African Americans in New York particularly hard, even though most were not clustered in the fields hit hardest by the downturn. July 13, 2009.

61. See Devin Friedman, "Will You Be My Black Friend?" *GQ*, November 2008 and Vanessa Grigoriadis, "Black and Blacker: The Racial Politics of the Obama Marriage," *New York*, August 10, 2008.

62. Michael Luo, "In Job Hunt, College Degree Can't Close Racial Gap," *New York Times*, December 1, 2009.

Index

A Note on the Author

WILLIAM JELANI COBB, Ph.D., is an associate professor and chair of the history department at Spelman College and was a delegate to the 2008 Democratic National Convention. He specializes in post–Civil War African American history, twentieth-century American politics, and the history of the Cold War. He is a contributing writer for *Essence* magazine, and his essays and reviews have appeared in the *Washington Post*, the *Progressive*, Alternet.org, and other publications. He has been a featured commentator on National Public Radio and CNN, in the acclaimed documentary *Beyond Beats & Rhymes*, and in other national outlets. He is the author of *To the Break of Dawn: A Freestyle on the Hip Hop Aesthetic* and *The Devil & Dave Chappelle and Other Essays*. He lives in Atlanta.